Daily Quizzes: Grammar and Sentence Structure
Grades 5 - 8

The Homeschool English Teacher
Abigail Hilson

Foreword by Las Vegas Mayor Carolyn Goodman

Education / Teaching / Materials & Devices

Daily Quizzes: Grammar and Sentence Structure
Grades 5 - 8

Part of The Homeschool English Teacher Series

www.TheHomeschoolEnglishTeacher.com

© 2023
Abigail Hilson
Las Vegas, NV USA

Cover Design: Olayemi Bolaji

Personal Dynamics Publishing
www.PersonalDynamicsPublishing.com

ISBN: 978-0-9890889-9-2

Dedication

To my family: avid readers, writers, and lovers of the English language.

Foreword

The importance of proper English grammar and usage can never be underestimated. Whether in the world of business or personal opportunity, there is never a substitute for a well-written document which has been completed through firsthand knowledge rather than through corrections and suggestions from sources in our technological world.

The materials in this book offer proven and time-honored resources to improve and review the fundamentals of English grammar. Abigail Hilson has condensed valuable insights from her years of teaching English into methods to learn how properly to compose sentences and to recognize correct grammar until it becomes second nature through repeated practice.

Carolyn Goodman

Mayor, City of Las Vegas

Contents

Section V: Adverbs

Section VI: Sentences

Preface – How To Use This Book

The purpose behind these short quizzes is to give parents / instructors / tutors a quick and easy assessment of the students' knowledge of basic concepts in grammar and the structure of sentences. They are designed to be given orally and then corrected together so that immediate reinforcement of the principles can be given. Ideally, quizzes could be given every day, but time constraints usually do not allow for that. As will be seen, these quizzes can be used to repeat the same challenges over and over again, day after day, until students have a thorough knowledge of the subject being tested. As with any assessment, some students will progress more quickly than others, but repetition is of the utmost importance.

Arranged in sections according to concepts, there are numerous quizzes so duplication is not an issue should a parent or instructor want to go back to review a subject covered earlier. It is possible to go to that section of quizzes and select one that was not used before. This allows for constant review of all principles. Most of the quizzes ask for only a one-word or a few-word answer so it is easy to give them on quarter sheets of scratch paper. Each quiz consists of only ten questions which makes correcting easy. If students know to expect a quiz on a regular basis, the process will move along smoothly, not take a great deal of time, and benefits will be noticeable.

Throughout the upcoming chapters, a few quizzes will have an asterisk (*). This denotes the quiz may be a little tricky in its lesson and may need a little more thought.

Abigail Hilson

The Homeschool English Teacher

Section I: NOUNS

Chapter 1: Recognizing Nouns

The following quizzes will review nouns. Included in this section will be review of numbers of nouns in a sentence, simple subjects, types of nouns, complements, plurals, and possessives.

In the first section, each quiz will consist of ten sentences containing one or more nouns. Students are to write the nouns on a piece of paper, and they will be shown in *italics* in the sentences for correcting purposes. The numbers in parentheses at the end of the sentences are the number of nouns the sentence contains. In the beginning it is sometimes helpful to let the students know how many nouns are in the sentence to help with recognition.

Quiz #1

1. The *dog* ran across the *grass* and through the *gate*. (3)

2. The *end* of the *movie* was a *surprise*. (3)

3. His *backpack*, *books*, and *binder* were on the *top* of the *locker*. (5)

4. *Freedom* is the *goal* of every *nation*. (3)

5. *Atlanta* was the host *city* for the *Olympics*. (3)

6. *Signs* of *sadness* appeared on her *face*. (3)

7. Her *ball* flew over the *fence* and landed in a *field*. (3)

8. A *crowd* of *people* had gathered on the *shore* of the *lake*. (4)

9. The *printer* on his *computer* was not hooked up to the correct *terminal*. (3)

10. A very large *pile* of *rock* was blocking the *entrance* to the narrow *canyon*. (4)

Note: Many of these quizzes can be varied by having students also identify the types of nouns involved. (Common, proper, abstract, or collective).

Quiz #2

1. His *impatience* caused them to receive a *penalty*. (2)

2. The top *half* of the large *continent* has a great *deal* of *humidity*. (4)

3. *Flocks* of *birds* in the *trees* announced the approaching *dawn*. (4)

4. He caught the *ball* overhead and threw it to second *base*. (2)

5. The *Sacramento River* overflowed its *banks* and flooded *houses, fields,* and *businesses*. (5)

6. The *players* on the *field* watched the *seconds* tick off the *clock*. (4)

7. The holiday *season* provided *time* for *parties* and delicious *food*. (4)

8. A *clock* on the *wall* struck the *hour* of *twelve*, and the *mice* ran back to their *holes*. (6)

9. Our *test* will cover the *parts* of *speech* and the *types* of *sentences*. (5)

10. The *flames* leaped up the *chimney*, and a warm *glow* filled the *room*. (4)

Quiz #3

1. The old *woman* fed bread *crumbs* to the *ducks* in the

park. (4)

2.   The *smile* on her *face* could not hide the *tears* in her *eyes.* (4)

3.   *Tons* of *water* rushed over the *falls* to the *pool* below. (4)

4.   The *people* on the *train* had a very enjoyable *trip.* (3)

5.   A sudden *brightness* in the evening *sky* caused many *people* to stop their *work.* (4)

6.   The *shock* of the good *news* was more than she could take. (2)

7.   We took *turns* playing in the *yard* with my little *sister.* (3)

8.   She examined the *test* with *care* before she answered a *question.* (3)

9.   The *stillness* of the *night* brought her *peace* and *comfort.* (4)

10. The *wind* whistled loudly through the large *grove* of *trees.* (3)

Quiz #4

1.   The *boy* in the *back* of the *room* asked his *teacher* a *question.* (5)

2.   That *test* on *Friday* covered the whole *chapter* and the *notes.* (4)

3.   The *animals* had a difficult *time* understanding the *change* in their *leader.* (4)

4.   The *happiness* of the *moment* brought *smiles* to all their *faces.* (4)

17

5.   After the *pig* had rolled in the *mud*, *Robert* gave her a *bath* before his evening *chores*. (5)

6.   The next *day* the *rain* had stopped, and the *sun* was brilliant in the blue *sky*. (4)

7.   *Liberty* is a most precious *gift*. (2)

8.   She will be going on a *trip* to *Los Angeles* on *Tuesday*. (3)

9.   The five *children* boarded the city *bus* and took a *seat* in the back *row*. (4)

10.   They will have the *experience* of a *lifetime* this *summer* on the archeological *dig* in *Colorado*. (5)

Quiz #5

1.   The three *boys* entered the last *house* on that *block*. (3)

2.   Tree *limbs* and other *debris* lay across *roads* and *sidewalks*. (4)

3.   She climbed to the *roof* of the *building* by the fire *escape*. (3)

4.   *Rulers* and *calculators* are needed for math *class* this *week*. (4)

5.   Many *flowers* bloomed in the *garden* by the *side* of my *house*. (4)

6.   The football *team* won its first *game* on *Saturday*. (3)

7.   Her *eyes* shone with *excitement* as her *father* outlined their next family *vacation*. (4)

8.   The *wind* roared over the *tops* of the *mountains* above the ski *resort*. (4)

9. The *papers* were in her *room* on her *desk*. (3)

10. A glorious *sunset* was the perfect *end* to a perfect *day*. (3)

Quiz #6

1. The *boys* and *girls* in my *class* were invited to the birthday *party*. (4)

2. The colorful *flowers* in our *garden* created an *atmosphere* of *brightness* and *cheer*. (5)

3. The new *lockers* were already in the *hallway* of the *school*. (3)

4. *Paper* and three *pencils* were required for the final *test* in our math *class.* (4)

5. New *books* and *workbooks* had been ordered by the *teacher* at the *end* of the *year*. (5)

6. The *weather* in *Las Vegas* is very warm in the *summer*. (3)

7. We could not find the *answer* to the *question* in the *index* of our *book*. (4)

8. *Cookies, candy*, and *donuts* were offered as a *part* of the *celebration* at *school* on *Friday*. (7)

9. The *officials* cleared the *floor*, and a first *score* came quickly in the first *minute* of the *game*. (5)

10. The *beauty* of the *landscape* captured the *attention* of the *photographer* and his *wife*. (5)

Quiz #7

1. A small glass *vase* was sitting on the *table* near the *door*. (3)

2.	The old *doctor* convinced his *friends* that the *water* had special *powers*. (4)

3.	Her *friendliness* was welcomed by the entire *group*. (2)

4.	The *score* of the *game* was never very close. (2)

5.	*Pots* and *pans* were piled high in the *sink*, but the *dishwasher* was empty. (4)

6.	I could not make any *sense* of the detailed *instructions*. (2)

7.	The *organizers* of the *event* forgot to deal with the unpredictable *weather*. (3)

8.	*Happiness* is the *key* to *success* and a long *life*. (4)

9.	The spotted *owl* at the *top* of the *tree* watched the *children* asleep below in their *tent*. (5)

10.	No one understood the *rules* so the *game* was not played well. (2)

Quiz #8

1.	The *lights* in the old *house* on the *corner* shone brightly. (3)

2.	He brought great *joy* to the *children* at *Christmas*. (3)

3.	The *test* in this *class* will be on *Friday*. (3)

4.	The beautiful *horse* entered the *barn* and walked to his *stall*. (3)

5.	*Books*, *pencils*, and *paper* were needed for the *survey* we were taking in *class*. (5)

6.	A *storm* moved across the *valley* and dropped *buckets* of *rain* on the small *town*. (5)

7. The *room* was filled with *excitement* at the *news* of her *promotion*. (4)

8. Three *jewels* in the *crown* sparkled in the bright *sunshine*. (3)

9. We went to the early *movie* at the *mall* with my *friend* and her *sister*. (4)

10. They crossed the rushing *brook* and entered a dark *forest* on the other *side*. (3)

Quiz #9

1. His *friends* arrived at his *house* for the *weekend*. (3)

2. Her *kindness* was appreciated by the entire *group*. (2)

3. *Tables* and *chairs* had been set up on the *floor* of the *gym*. (4)

4. *Sue* and my *sister* spent the entire *day* at the *mall*. (4)

5. My five *books* are due at the *library* on *Tuesday*. (3)

6. New *paintings* and *drawings* were in the *hall* by the main *entrance*. (4)

7. *Friendship* is a *key* to *happiness*. (3)

8. A raging *storm* kept them in the *house* for the entire *weekend*. (3)

9. She brought her *grades* up by the *end* of the *quarter*. (3)

10. A large *pack* of *dogs* was roaming the *streets* looking for *food*. (4)

Quiz #10

1. The *surprise* of the *moment* could be heard in her *voice*. (3)

2. A new *day* began with fluffy white *clouds* appearing over the *mountains*. (3)

3. Several *boats* were docked along the *shores* of the *Mississippi River*. (3)

4. Each *boy* brought a *friend* to the birthday *party* at the *park* down the *street*. (5)

5. A large *string* of colorful *lights* circles every *house* in our *neighborhood*. (4)

6. The dark *curtains* created an *atmosphere* of *gloom*. (3)

7. A *flock* of *geese* rose from the *pond* in our *field*. (4)

8. *Honesty* and *integrity* are two *traits* all *people* admire. (4)

9. Election *day* is a big *event* for *television*. (3)

10. He leaned out the *window* and called to his *friend*. (2)

Quiz #11

1. He left his *books* and *binders* in his *locker*. (3)

2. The *girl* could hear loud *music* coming from the *house*. (3)

3. It takes *courage* to admit your *mistakes*. (2)

4. An eager *audience* applauded her *performance* on *Saturday*. (3)

5. A *break* in the *weather* allowed the *race* to continue. (3)

6. *Tables* and *chairs* were stacked in every *corner* of the large *room*. (4)

7. That *author* wrote numerous *poems* and *essays*. (3)

8. The yellow *wallpaper* came off the bedroom *wall* in *strips*. (3)

9. *Minneapolis* is the twin *city* to *St. Paul*. (3)

10. *Wisdom* is a *tool* for *strength* and *success*. (4)

Quiz #12

1. A very loud *noise* in the *night* attracted their *attention*. (3)

2. The small *room* was filled with *children* and *adults*. (3)

3. We brought *games*, *decorations*, and *refreshments* for the *party*. (4)

4. *Peace* on *Earth* is a *wish* often expressed at holiday *time*. (4)

5. She ran quickly down the *hall* to get her *assignment* from her *locker*. (3)

6. *Sweaters*, *jackets*, and *hats* were hanging on *hooks* against the back *wall*. (5)

7. Her *hair* sparkled in the *light* of the bright *moon*. (3)

8. Dry *leaves* blew across the *field* as the *wind* increased. (3)

9. They leave for *school* on *Friday*. (2)

10. The *end* of the *story* brought *sadness* to all of the *children* in the *room*. (5)

Quiz #13

1. My three *friends* approached the dark *mansion* very cautiously. (2)

2. The *workers* took a *break* for a morning *snack*. (3)

3. Her *emotions* could not be contained in the *thrill* of the *moment*. (3)

4. That surprising *announcement* filled his *face* with *amazement*. (3)

5. *Candy* and *cookies* were in a large *bowl* by the front *door*. (4)

6. All of the committee *members* shook *hands* with the *men* on the *panel*. (4)

7. *Green* and *gold* were the *colors* selected for the *event*. (4)

8. A warm *coat*, *mittens*, and a *scarf* were on the *bench* in the *hall* by the *door*. (6)

9. His *notebook* was left on the *counter* in the *kitchen*. (3)

10. The *children* walked quickly down *Dove Street* toward their father's *office*. (3)

Quiz #14

1. The *sun* shone through the open *window* and provided *warmth*. (3)

2. He was filled with *pride* at his *name* on the special *list*. (3)

3. A huge *box* contained *clothes* and other *items* for the *shelter*. (4)

4. On *Halloween* my little *brother* was a *pirate* with a

colorful *parrot*. (4)

5. The strong *wind* blew the *branches* of the *trees* against the *house*. (4)

6. Everyone wanted a *position* on my sister's *team*. (2)

7. The *test* in math *class* was difficult without a *calculator*. (3)

8. She applied *pressure* to the *glue* to hold the broken *piece* in its *place*. (4)

9. His *loyalty* was appreciated by other *members* of the *club*. (3)

10. I shall return the *books* to the *library* after my *report*. (3)

Quiz #15

1. *Stacks* of *cups* and *saucers* had been placed on the *table* near the coffee *dispenser*. (5)

2. She carefully carried the glass *vase* from the *study* to the kitchen *counter*. (3)

3. Our *gardener* planted *daisies* and *roses* in the flower *beds* near the *porch*. (5)

4. Everyone will need a *pencil* and a *calculator* for the math *test* in the *morning*. (4)

5. Her birthday *party* will be on Saturday *afternoon*. (2)

6. My *mother* will send an *invitation* to each *student* in my *class*. (4)

7. Dark gray *clouds* covered the *sky* as the *rain* began to fall. (3)

8. Your library *books* are due on *Thursday*. (2)

9. *Carrots* and *onions* were added to the *stew* as it

simmered on the *stove*. (4)

10. We decided to take a *hike* on the *trail* along the *river*. (3)

Quiz #16

1. The *girls* brought *cookies* and *brownies* for the bake *sale*. (4)

2. A *look* of *pride* came over her *parents* at the *announcement* of the *winners*. (5)

3. There were many *birds* in the *trees* in our *yard*. (3)

4. Several *books* were missing from his *collection*. (2)

5. Powerful *waves* hit the *beach*, sending *spray* into the *air*. (4)

6. The small *child* was overcome with *emotion* at the *sight* of his *gifts*. (4)

7. Bright *packages* lay beneath the lovely *tree*. (2)

8. A high *wall* surrounded the *park* and *playground*. (3)

9. A *bouquet* of *flowers* sat on the *table* in the large *lobby*. (4)

10. The *freshness* of the early morning *air* brought *color* to her *cheeks*. (4)

Quiz #17

1. The small *rabbits* ran through the *meadow* of tall *grass*. (3)

2. *Saturday* is his *birthday*, and his *mother* is giving a *party*. (4)

3. Our *team* will fly to *Houston* at the *end* of the *week*. (4)

4. Her *voice* quavered as *tears* rolled down her *cheeks*. (3)

5. *Books*, *paper*, and *pens* tumbled out of the *locker* onto the *floor*. (5)

6. Her *homework* took a large *bite* out of the *weekend*. (3)

7. The *plane* taxied down the *runway* toward the *terminal*. (3)

8. Her *expression* of pure *delight* thrilled the *audience*. (3)

9. *Sue* and *Nancy* are going with us to the *mall* and the *movie*. (4)

10. Her *eyes* were as big as *saucers* when she saw her new *doll*. (3)

Quiz #18

1. His *impatience* raised the *level* of the group's *frustration*. (3)

2. She had done the *cover* of the *book* in very bright *colors*. (3)

3. My *mother* is baking *cookies*, *muffins*, and *crepes* for the *celebration*. (5)

4. The small *boy* walked cautiously down the long *hall*. (2)

5. A large *crowd* gathered around the *stage* to show *support* for the *candidate*. (4)

6. We are taking our *vacation* in *San Francisco* this *summer*. (3)

7. Brilliant *gems* caught the *sun* in the display *case* at the jewelry *store*. (4)

8. *Students* are required to conduct *experiments* and prepare *labs* in *science*. (4)

9. *Participation* in the *event* became a real *challenge*. (3)

10. *Anger* and *fear* came over the lost *child* as *night* approached. (4)

Quiz #19

1. My *parents* took us to *Europe* over the *summer*. (3)

2. Small *children* stood in the long *line* for a *ride* on the *train*. (4)

3. A large *basket* of *candy* had been placed by the front *door*. (3)

4. A dark *column* of *smoke* rose in the clear, blue *sky*. (3)

5. Each *day* the *library* orders *hundreds* of *newspapers*. (4)

6. *Parents* and *teachers* met in the *auditorium* to plan the *event*. (4)

7. We could not see the *bridge* because of the *fog*. (2)

8. A large *pile* of *paper* had been stacked in the *center* of the *desk*. (4)

9. She begins her *day* with a *cup* of *coffee* and a blueberry *muffin*. (4)

10. Bad *weather* threatened to ruin their camping *trip*. (2)

Quiz #20

1. The *boys* went with their *friends* to a *movie*. (3)

2. His *anger* was obvious to all *members* of the *group*. (3)

3. The *author* of that *story* we read in *class* is *Mark Twain*. (4)

4. A *ladder* stretched to the *roof* of the storage *shed*. (3)

5. My *sister* and her best *friend* have the same *birthday*. (3)

6. The *excitement* of the *moment* could be heard in the *cheering* of the *audience*. (4)

7. She left her *house* and went to the grocery *store*. (2)

8. The *mountain* glistened in the last *rays* of the setting summer *sun*. (3)

9. A small *table* and four *chairs* were placed in the *hall* by the *door*. (4)

10. The *river* had risen two *feet* in the *time* that we watched from the *bridge*. (4)

Quiz #21

1. The *men* laid new *carpet* in the *bedroom* and the *hall*. (4)

2. We read two *stories* today in English *class*. (2)

3. Her *patience* was rewarded by the eventual *appearance* of her *son*. (3)

4. A very bright *light* shone from the bedroom *window*. (2)

5. A new school *bus* was parked at the *end* of the *street*. (3)

6. He quickly grabbed a *pencil*, *paper*, and a *calculator*

from his *locker*. (4)

7. A loud *noise* stopped him in his *tracks*. (2)

8. A *pile* of *books* was on the coffee *table* near the *sofa*. (4)

9. One twinkling *star* rose in the evening *sky*. (2)

10. The *highway* was planted with *bushes*, *trees*, and *flowers*. (4)

Chapter 2: Simple Subjects

In the following quizzes, students will be writing the simple subject of each sentence. Some simple subjects in this section will be pronouns instead of nouns. Simple subjects are single words (unless they are proper nouns), do not have to be at the beginning of the sentence, are **never** found in phrases, and are the understood pronoun "you" in imperative sentences. The simple subject of a sentence can always be found by asking "who" or "what" in front of the verb. The answers will be shown in italics, and students will write the simple subjects on their papers.

Quiz #1

1. Why did that *man* on horseback drop out of the parade?

2. Through all the shouting and cheering, my father's *voice* could still be heard.

3. At the end of the avenue stood the *Lincoln Memorial*.

4. With his friends from school, my *brother* hopes to make the local team.

5. The *ice* in the frosty mug was melting rapidly.

6. Did the new *boy* in my class come to school today?

7. Near the back of the house was a *flight* of stairs.

8. The *paint* on the wall was chipping and flaking.

9. By the door to his bedroom lay a neat *stack* of Sunday morning newspapers.

10. The *bells* in the church rang loudly during the lunch hour.

Quiz #2

1. From the valley at the base of the mountain rose a *column* of black smoke.

2. Take out the trash, please.   (*You*)

3. On the opposite side of the field, our nervous *coach* was pacing up and down.

4. An unopened *bottle* of soda lay on the kitchen table.

5. Will the whole *group* of boys be going?

6. Show me how to solve this problem.   (*You*)

7. The lonely old *man* sat quietly on the bench in the shade.

8. *He* brought the broken chair in for repairs.

9. A thick *blanket* of clouds covered the towers of the bridge.

10. On the table by the entrance were three *vases* of flowers.

Quiz #3

1. The young *boy* stood silently on the bridge.

2. By the door to the gym, three basketball *players* waited for their coach.

3. *Sam Johnson* won the starting position easily.

4. Did your oldest *sister* enter the contest?

5. On the steps of the deserted school sat a large, black *dog*.

6. *Most* of the boys will be leaving tomorrow.

7. By the edge of the lake, the *wind* was blowing steadily.

8.   *Niagara Falls* is a popular tourist attraction.

9.   That *man* in the dark suit entered the room behind us.

10. The *sound* of thunder could be heard in the distance.

Quiz #4

1.   The fuzzy brown *kitten* playfully chased its tail.

2.   At the concert *Tom Miller* introduced us to his friends in the band.

3.   A large *stack* of papers sat on the corner of the desk.

4.   Near the middle of the lake swam three beautiful *swans*.

5.   *He* asked politely for a sheet of paper.

6.   Down the street by our house, a black *car* cruised slowly.

7.   Run to the store for some milk.   (*You*)

8.   On the door a large *sign* had been hung.

9.   The *flowers* in the garden were blooming beautifully.

10. In my last class of the day, a fire *drill* was planned.

Quiz #5

1.   At the back of the room stood a tall *man* in a dark coat.

2.   A small *bottle* of juice was on the kitchen table.

3.   On the top of the desk, a huge *box* of crayons was visible.

4.   Get me a paper towel, please.   (*You*)

5.   At the end of our street lives an old *man* with twelve cats.

6.   In the hallway the *librarian* was sorting books for the sale.

7.   A thick *cloud* of dust filled the morning sky.

8.   Did the other *coach* call your name?

9.   A large *bag* of chips blew off the picnic table.

10.   When will the basketball *practice* be over?

Quiz #6

Remember: "There" can never be a subject

1.   By our cabin the *water* around the edge of the lake was frozen.

2.   There were six new *members* on our soccer team.

3.   Standing at the edge of the sidewalk were three *policemen*.

4.   The small *package* of pencils was still on the counter.

5.   By the end of the evening, the *committee* had selected a winner.

6.   On the streets at rush hour, there is always *traffic*.

7.   A very large *glass* of water sat on her nightstand.

8.   Near the door to the barn were three *pails* of fresh milk.

9.   The *pleasure* of his company was enough for them.

10.   Over the pounding of the rain could be heard the *howling* of the wind.

Quiz #7

1. Around the sharp corner in the road came a speeding red *car*.

2. Five *members* of our club received prizes.

3. A fine *cover* of white clouds lay over the tops of the high mountains.

4. Send me all the information on that subject. (*You*)

5. Couldn't the *lady* in the ticket office find your order?

6. On her dining room table lay a brand new *set* of dishes.

7. The *discovery* of gold in California caused a rush to the West.

8. In the parlor car of the train, the *windows* were darkened for sleep.

9. Please run these *recipes* over to your mother. (*You*)

10. The small *canary* in the cage sang a soft, sweet song.

Quiz #8

1. Didn't the *coach* of the tennis team plan an afternoon match?

2. On the railing of the porch perched three white *doves*.

3. The *edge* of the lake was lined with water lilies.

4. When will the second *bell* ring?

5. Can't the *members* of our committee meet tonight?

6. The *ice* on the surface of the puddle had melted in the sun.

7. A *bowl* of apples was on the table.

8. Please return to the store for some milk. (*You*)

9. Three small *sheets* of paper fluttered to the floor.

10. Around our corner at full speed came three police *cars*.

Quiz #9

1. In the center of the village, a *group* of children sang carols.

2. Suddenly, a very startled *kitten* darted from the bushes.

3. On the foot of the bed lay a gorgeous red *gown*.

4. *All* of the students on the team were invited to the event.

5. There were many tropical *flowers* in her garden.

6. The *roofs* of all the houses were covered with snow.

7. Over the nearby mountains came an extremely powerful *storm*.

8. On the other side of the road, a large *cloud* of dust rose from the field.

9. A huge *pile* of wood had been gathered for the bonfire.

10. Here is a *list* of the supplies for the party.

Quiz #10

1. A good *friend* of mine will be coming with us.

2. Close to the edge of the stream nested two *owls*.

3. Do not forget the bread. (*You*)

4. The small *group* of musicians will play on Saturday.

5. A glass *pitcher* of milk stood near the edge of the table.

6. The soft *sound* of a church bell could be heard in the distance.

7. Try that delicious dessert. (*You*)

8. A long *line* of students waited for tickets to the game.

9. Over the tops of the trees flew two rescue *helicopters*.

10. *Everyone* could hear the music from the street.

Quiz #11

1. On the field a large *flock* of geese had landed.

2. Take the dirty dishes to the sink, please. (*You*)

3. Around the campfire gathered the *counselors* for the camp.

4. The tall *man* in the gray suit is the featured speaker.

5. A brand new *carton* of eggs was placed on the kitchen counter.

6. At the back of the auditorium, *everyone* waited for the program to begin.

7. Clean your room before the party. (*You*)

8. A loud *bell* at the top of the steeple rang the hour.

9. In the highest branch of the pine tree appeared a bald *eagle*.

10. The *bottle* of juice crashed to the floor.

Quiz #12

1. At the very top of the slope waited three anxious *skiers*.

2. By four o'clock the *cars* had left the stadium parking lot.

3. Close the door quickly. (*You*)

4. At the back of the court, the *members* of our team waited patiently.

5. The *tops* of the trees swayed in the breeze.

6. A dark *column* of smoke rose from the roof of the garage.

7. There were three tiny *puppies* in a basket by the fire.

8. Here are the *instructions* for the project.

9. Turn out the lights at nine o'clock. (*You*)

10. On the tower the *hands* of the giant clock moved quite slowly.

Quiz #13

1. By the small white fence grew some lovely *roses*.

2. A *group* of students came for the special presentation.

3. At the back of the house, my *father* has built a small storage shed.

4. Could the *winner* of the race come to the photography booth?

5. There were three *bags* of candy on the shelf.

6. Two very small *kittens* scampered around the yard.

7. Run to the fence and back. (*You*)

38

8. In the conference room, the *members* of the committee selected a president.

9. A bright *light* spread dark shadows across the field.

10. Near the back of the room was arranged a *row* of chairs.

Quiz #14

1. Out of the house walked my *brother* with our dog.

2. A fierce *gust* of wind carried the lawn chairs across the patio.

3. From the end of the field hobbled our injured *quarterback*.

4. By the rose bush in our yard, the tiny *puppy* buried his bone.

5. Last night the *leader* of our band called a late rehearsal.

6. After school my *sister* should have called home.

7. Before the game the *girls* on our team practiced for an hour.

8. In a neat row by the window sat ten new *computers*.

9. In the clubhouse before the game, the *cheerleaders* rehearsed their new routine.

10. A new *list* of names was compiled before the trip.

Quiz #15

1. By the flagpole on the corner paced a spotted, brown and white *dog*.

2. There were three *winners* in the contest.

3. Near the shore of the lake, two small *children* played.

4. The *dishes* on the table were beautiful.

5. In the meadow stood an old, thatched *hut*.

6. Will the final *race* begin in an hour?

7. Toward the end of the three-hour practice, the *players* were extremely tired.

8. In the backyard my *father* was barbecuing steaks.

9. There will be a *group* of parents near the far door.

10. Several stormy, gray *clouds* rose above the hills.

Quiz #16

1. Across the room walked four confident young *women*.

2. The *boys* in the jazz band played very well.

3. Down the hallway a loud *series* of shouts could be heard.

4. Over the outfielder's head flew the *ball*.

5. A giant *stack* of library books was near the door of the classroom.

6. *Five* of the players on my team had the flu.

7. In the tiny garden near the fence sprouted several new *vegetables*.

8. During the night a tremendous *fire* raged in the dense forest.

9. Please find a hammer and some nails.   (*You*)

10. From the bottom locker came the distinct *odor* of decaying food.

Quiz #17

1.   By the side of the road was parked an empty *van*.

2.   *Thousands* of geese had landed on the sparkling lake.

3.   In the middle of the auditorium, a *group* of students was decorating the tree.

4.   Suddenly, a loud *crash* came from the roof.

5.   A large *bouquet* of flowers had arrived in the office.

6.   Where will the *supplies* be delivered?

7.   From behind the curtain on the stage came a muffled *cry*.

8.   His organizational *skills* are extremely lacking.

9.   On the long serving table, a *block* of ice had been sculpted into a turkey.

10.   The committee *chairman* selected another member for the board.

Quiz #18

1.   After their performance the *girls* in the choir went to the movies.

2.   From the wide mouth of the cave flew *hundreds* of bats.

3.   How soon can the *children* return to the classroom?

4.   In the center of the table was a *bowl* of cherries.

5.   Along the fence the *gardeners* had planted rose bushes.

6.   From behind the curtain in the next room floated a soft piano *solo*.

7. Will the next *participant* in the event please step forward?

8. Out of the north a blustery *wind* blew across the open plains.

9. Before the first light of dawn, the *race* had begun.

10. Many *rows* of chairs had been placed across the front of the auditorium.

Quiz #19

1. Over the noise of the carpenters, there was a high-pitched *whistle*.

2. The *players* on my team voted for the Saturday practice.

3. In the basket near the front door lay my mother's *keys*.

4. What game did our *team* win?

5. On the shelf in the garage stood three large *containers* of nails.

6. By Friday afternoon our *project* was completed.

7. The *edge* of the lake had frozen during the night.

8. Four *bottles* of colored ink had disappeared from the storage closet.

9. The *call* of the umpire saved him at home plate.

10. In the trunk in the hall, my *mother* found my missing coat.

Quiz #20

1. Through the mountain meadow ran a sparkling *brook*.

2. A full *carton* of eggs had been left on the shelf by the door.

3. *Many* of the children had forgotten their lunches.

4. In a new suit and dress shoes, the young *man* appeared very confident.

5. From across the large field came a frightening *shout*.

6. The small *boy* with his red wagon was selling lemonade around the neighborhood.

7. A bright *beam* of white light pierced the black sky.

8. Some *members* of the band must attend the meeting.

9. In the center of the ring, a clever *magician* was performing tricks.

10. At the park *everyone* wanted a turn on the monster slide.

Quiz #21

1. In the stream the *salmon* were fighting against the current.

2. From the edge of the stage, the *orchestra* played its piece.

3. Every *person* in the audience enjoyed the concert.

4. By the end of the day, committee *members* were exhausted.

5. Isn't *New York* the largest city in the country?

6. There were four large *crows* sitting in the top of the oak tree.

7. Can't the *coach* of the team arrange for transportation?

8.   By the side of the road was parked an abandoned *car*.

9.   At the game on Saturday, the *president* of our club received an award.

10.   A grizzly *bear* wandered slowly into camp.

Quiz #22

1.   By the end of the day, the *students* had completed the project.

2.   A dense *blanket* of fog covered the city all day.

3.   Around the package was tied a blue and yellow *ribbon*.

4.   A gigantic *pile* of leaves had been raked into the street.

5.   Can't *both* of my brothers come, too?

6.   Near the back door of the shop were piled six *boxes* of books.

7.   *Most* of the crowd had already left the stadium.

8.   At the front of the room, there was a small *table* for registration.

9.   The young *girl* could not get her cold hands into the mittens.

10.   From the top of the tower, a loud *bell* sounded the hour.

Quiz #23

1.   A *bundle* of newspapers was stacked in the attic.

2.   From a window of the haunted house came a mournful *scream*.

3.   Very carefully, the young *boy* found his way through the maze.

4.   A beautiful *song* could be heard in the auditorium.

5.   Many ominous, dark *clouds* hung over the valley.

6.   A *feeling* of excitement spread through the children in line.

7.   Down the rushing river moved *debris* from the flooding.

8.   On the field the *members* of the team anxiously awaited the ruling.

9.   Into the dark room floated a shrouded *figure*.

10.   Three *rows* of chairs were arranged near the stage.

Quiz #24

1.   Three *groups* of boys were waiting for the bus.

2.   Along the dusty trail slowly moved an overloaded *wagon*.

3.   Toward the end of the day, a *line* of dark clouds was approaching the valley.

4.   Five energetic *puppies* raced around the enclosed yard.

5.   A large *box* of crayons sat on the kitchen counter.

6.   Near the mouth of the small lake landed six white *geese*.

7.   Suddenly, the loud *blast* of a horn pierced the silent darkness.

8.   The young *man* showed a great deal of courage.

9.   From the far end of the deserted stadium came a *shout*.

10. In the woods near our cabin, a *pack* of wolves howled through the night air.

Quiz #25

1. Ten *cans* of soda were lined up on the counter.

2. With the first breeze of autumn, the colored *leaves* began to fall.

3. Last Saturday my *sister* ordered a new dress for the prom.

4. Carry your clothes upstairs, please.   (*You*)

5. The *boys* on the team congratulated their captain.

6. At the edge of the woods ran a well-used deer *trail*.

7. Will the *members* of the team arrive on time?

8. Yesterday, my best *friend* called from California.

9. Return your books to the library.   (*You*)

10. On the desk in the corner sat a brand new *computer*.

Quiz #26

1. Around the corner a new *store* had just opened.

2. Down the windy tracks of the steep mountain crept the long *train*.

3. A *bundle* of newspapers was thrown on the porch.

4. Three *members* of the band will perform on Saturday.

5. In the middle of the playground stood a huge *dog*.

6. The dry *leaves* on the trees rustled in the wind.

7. Turn in your work on time.   (*You*)

8. A whole *bag* of assorted candy lay on the checkout stand.

9. On the downtown bus, a young *man* examined the paper closely.

10. The *books* on the table were from his library.

Quiz #27

1. The *members* of the club elected a president.

2. Over the tops of the hills came a *line* of soldiers.

3. Stop at the gate. (*You*)

4. A large *block* of ice jammed the creek.

5. Down the center of the meadow flowed a clear *stream*.

6. The *boys* in the band performed at the park.

7. Four *girls* from my class entered the contest.

8. Two *rows* of corn were planted in the garden.

9. Turn to the left. (*You*)

10. On the top of the tree was perched an *eagle*.

Quiz #28

1. By the side of the road, a yellow *van* was parked.

2. There were several *students* in the room.

3. At the edge of the freeway grew a *row* of trees.

4. The *participants* in the group baked dozens of cookies.

5. Run to the store. (*You*)

6. Out of the corner of the room emerged a small *child*.

7. The *blinds* on each window were closed.

8. In the front of the pet store lay a tiny *puppy*.

9. A bright *beam* of light shone through the upper window.

10. That large *group* of girls will be participating in the event.

Quiz #29

1. On the trees the *squirrels* scampered playfully in the afternoon sun.

2. At the top of the hill, the *skiers* in the race waited patiently.

3. A huge *flock* of geese had landed during the night.

4. From the kitchen floated the rich *aroma* of our dinner.

5. On the pages of the encyclopedia were colorful *pictures* of animals.

6. The large *load* of boxes fell from the bed of the truck.

7. In the royal carriage, the *queen* sat proudly.

8. The *noise* from the train woke our guests.

9. In the shade of the old oak tree rested two small *dogs*.

10. A thick *blanket* of fog lay over the city.

Quiz #30

1. In the heavy rain, the nervous *man* drove to the station.

2. The new *desks* were lined up along the wall.

3. At the edge of the forest stood a frightened *deer*.

4. Above the sound of the wind, an eerie *whistle* could be heard.

5. A beautiful white *swan* swam in the middle of the lake.

6. Into the room walked my *friends* from school.

7. Her fancy *printer* sat next to her desk.

8. For the festival in the park, my brother's *band* performed.

9. Down the road from the center of town came three large *trucks*.

10. By the end of the day, my *homework* is always completed.

Quiz #31

1. Over the entrance to the cave hung large *sheets* of plastic.

2. A beautiful *bouquet* of flowers was on the table.

3. At the very top of the pine tree sat a huge spotted *owl*.

4. Four heavy *books* fell from the bookcase in my room.

5. On the bulletin board by the office, the *secretary* posted the new schedule.

6. At the bottom of the locker, her *lunch* was completely smashed.

7. The *pilots* in the group discussed their travel plans.

8. Near the back of the room paced a very anxious *father*.

9. The large *bag* of groceries toppled off of the counter.

10. A colorful hot-air *balloon* rose over the stadium.

Quiz #32

1. Three young *ladies* walked toward the court.

2. In the middle of the field was a small *herd* of sheep.

3. Please put the books back on the table.   (*You*)

4. Several *chairs* were left in the hall.

5. The computer *screen* displayed a new menu.

6. From the end of the hallway came a very loud *noise*.

7. In the basket by the fireplace sat six small *kittens*.

8. There was an *article* about that in the newspaper.

9. My *friends* arrived at 3 o'clock.

10. A large *column* of ants marched across the garden.

Chapter 3: Complements

In the following quizzes, students will be writing the complements from each sentence. There are four different kinds of complements, *predicate nominatives, predicate adjectives, direct objects, and indirect objects*, and all will be represented in these quizzes even though this is the noun section. The majority of complements are nouns or pronouns; therefore, this is the most logical section for practicing their usage.

Remember: Predicate nominatives and predicate adjectives always take a linking verb.

The complements will be shown in italics and their type in parentheses at the end of the sentence. The students will be asked to identify the word in italics.

Quiz #1

These first quizzes do not contain any predicate *adjectives*.

1.   The architect gave my *parents* the new plans. (indirect object)

2.   What *gift* did you receive?   (direct object)

3.   She will soon be the last *contestant*.   (pred. nominative)

4.   The board offered the *members* another solution. (indirect object)

5.   The biggest problem is the *ants*.   (pred. nominative)

6.   A blanket of snow covered the *yard*.   (direct object)

7.   I sent my *sister* a letter.   (indirect object)

8.   They could not find any *gifts* at the last minute. (direct object)

9.   At the mall we sang Christmas *carols* for a week. (direct object)

10. The light drizzle was not a steady *downpour*. (pred. nominative)

Quiz #2

1.   He borrowed three baseball *bats* from the coach. (direct object)

2.   They were following a windy *path* through the forest. (direct object)

3.   My friend should have been the *winner*.   (pred. nominative)

4.   We sent my *mother* flowers at the hospital. (indirect object)

5.   Mary has removed her *name* from the list.   (direct object)

6.   The new girl has become a top *student*.   (pred. nominative)

7.   The organizers offered the *volunteers* refreshments. (indirect object)

8.   She ordered her *father* a new watch.   (indirect object)

9.   The boys stacked the *logs* against the fence.   (direct object)

10. The weather was the only *inconvenience* of the trip. (pred. nominative)

Quiz #3

1. He will buy more *milk* tomorrow. (direct object)

2. My mother brought *Sue* a very warm jacket. (indirect object)

3. The captain has become the best *player* on the team. (pred. nominative)

4. The tornado caused much *destruction*. (direct object)

5. His father is the new scout *leader*. (pred. nominative)

6. He even wore a *suit* for the festivities. (direct object)

7. They asked the *teacher* many questions. (indirect object)

8. The announcer called her *name* as the winner. (direct object)

9. My grandmother handed my *brother* a special gift. (indirect object)

10. Will the new club president be *Mr. Grant*? (pred. nominative)

Quiz #4

1. The man on the stage is my *father*. (pred. nominative)

2. She rode her new *bicycle* to the mall. (direct object)

3. The small child brought his *sister* some flowers. (indirect object)

4. The gym is now our *cafeteria*. (pred. nominative)

5. They heard a loud *crash* from behind the door. (direct object)

6. Please give my *friend* a piece of cake. (indirect object)

7. She became the *champion* of that event. (pred. nominative)

8. My brother mailed *Sam* a package from Europe. (indirect object)

9. She entered the *room* quietly. (direct object)

10. They called his *name* over the loudspeaker. (direct object)

Quiz #5

1. The snowball hit the *window*. (direct object)

2. He loudly called his *dog* in from the yard. (direct object)

3. That girl was obviously the *winner*. (pred. nominative)

4. The waitress brought the *lady* a sandwich. (indirect object)

5. Frank has already been the *captain* of our team. (pred. nominative)

6. The young man gave his *friend* flowers. (indirect object)

7. No one saw the old *man* on the corner. (direct object)

8. The whole team could have been the *stars* of the game. (pred. nominative)

9. I recently sent my *mother* a letter. (indirect object)

10. She answered the *telephone* in the kitchen. (direct object)

Quiz #6

1. He loaded the *groceries* for his mother. (direct object)

2. My father showed *Shelley* the location on the map. (indirect object)

3. Those two boys are my *cousins*. (pred. nominative)

4. She has finally become a famous *actress.* (pred. nominative)

5. The man dragged the *log* across the yard. (direct object)

6. She placed three *dishes* upon the counter. (direct object)

7. Her mother baked the whole *class* cookies. (indirect object)

8. My sister will be the *star* of the program. (pred. nominative)

9. The man gave the little *boy* the three candy canes. (indirect object)

10. They created a beautiful *design* on paper. (direct object)

Quiz #7

The following quizzes contain all four types of complements.

1. My friend brought her *classmates* cookies for

Christmas.   (indirect object)

2. No one wanted the *leftovers* from last night's dinner. (direct object)

3. My sister has become the assistant basketball *coach*. (pred. nominative)

4. Your mother will be bringing your *books* to school. (direct object)

5. He was extremely *tired* after practice.   (pred. adjective)

6. My parents sent my *brother* his presents last week. (indirect object)

7. The panel selected three *contestants* for the final event.   (direct object)

8. That was *Sally*.   (pred. nominative)

9. She was feeling very *lonely* in the big, empty house. (pred. adjective)

10. The coach ordered the *team* new jerseys.   (indirect object)

Quiz #8

1. Almost every week we buy *vegetables* at the produce market.   (direct object)

2. Will you please bring the *cookies* to my house? (direct object)

3. The whole group seemed extremely *weary* after the trip.   (pred. adjective)

4. The streets had become *rivers* in the heavy rain. (pred. nominative)

5. My mother sewed *him* a great costume for

Halloween.   (indirect object)

6.   She was quite *upset* with our whole group.   (pred. adjective)

7.   The new time schedule created a *problem* for them. (direct object)

8.   He will always by my best *catcher* on the team. (pred. nominative)

9.   The teacher always gives the *students* a test on Friday.   (indirect object)

10.   A mother swan quietly led her *family* away from the boaters.   (direct object)

Quiz #9

1.   Each weekend my brother gives the *dog* a bath. (indirect object)

2.   She could easily become my best *friend*.   (pred. nominative)

3.   They carefully removed the *labels* from each jar. (direct object)

4.   After winning first place, she was very *proud*. (pred. adjective)

5.   The screen on my computer seems too *dark*. (pred. adjective)

6.   The school was ordering the *library* several new books.   (indirect object)

7.   My younger sister is also a *mother* of four.   (pred. nominative)

8.   The team has defeated every other division *member*. (direct object)

9. The sky overhead looked *gloomy*.   (pred. adjective)

10. The three boys rode their *bikes* to the park.   (direct object)

Quiz #10

1. After the show we bought *donuts* at the mall. (direct object)

2. Will you send my *friend* the photos?   (indirect object)

3. We ran the last *mile* in the rain.   (direct object)

4. My very best friend seems *lonely*.   (pred. adjective)

5. The carpenters were hammering *nails* into the frame. (direct object)

6. Please bring my *class* some good news.   (indirect object)

7. That team was last year's *champions*.   (pred. nominative)

8. Everyone in the event received a *ribbon*.   (direct object)

9. The new student can be your *partner*.   (pred. nominative)

10. Can they mail my *mother* the forms?   (indirect object)

Quiz #11

1. My mother grows *vegetables* in the garden.   (direct object)

2. George is the *chairman* of the committee.   (pred. nominative)

3.   We will run a *marathon* on Saturday. (direct object)

4.   Please mail the *letters* today. (direct object)

5.   He felt very *nervous* about his new assignment. (pred. adjective)

6.   Was my friend the *winner* of the contest? (pred. nominative)

7.   She soon became the *star* of the show. (pred. nominative)

8.   The boy carried the *groceries* into the house. (direct object)

9.   Did she seem *quiet* during the discussion? (pred. adjective)

10.   The man drove the *bus* slowly past our house. (direct object)

Quiz #12

1.   My mother gave *Sue* the last piece of cake. (indirect object)

2.   The practices after school were an absolute *necessity*. (pred. nominative)

3.   He watered the numerous *plants* in the garden. (direct object)

4.   The vet put a tiny *collar* around my cat's neck. (direct object)

5.   My brother sent the *university* his application. (indirect object)

6.   Our football team was *unbeaten*. (pred. adjective)

7.   Her friend is often the *leader* on hikes. (pred. nominative)

8. Nathan Hale gave his *life* for his country. (direct object)

9. The new position brought the young *man* responsibility. (indirect object)

10. They searched the entire *playground* for the missing button. (direct object)

Quiz #13

1. The Declaration of Independence is a national *treasure*. (pred. nominative)

2. My mother bought a new *jacket* for my brother. (direct object)

3. Her sister became the homecoming *queen* at the prom. (pred. nominative)

4. I faxed my *friends* the notes from history. (indirect object)

5. During the morning we loaded *hundreds* of boxes. (direct object)

6. She baked her *class* gingerbread men. (indirect object)

7. His most popular songs have become *timeless*. (pred. adjective)

8. Over the winter the town supplied the *army* with food. (direct object)

9. The strong wind blew the remaining *leaves* from the tree. (direct object)

10. We always bring the *homeless* clothes for the winter. (indirect object)

Quiz #14

1.   The committee purchased *cookies* for the meeting. (direct object)

2.   She has become very *talented*. (pred. adjective)

3.   We ordered a large *pizza* for our study session. (direct object)

4.   My brother sent his *girlfriend* a birthday card. (indirect object)

5.   Should they be the new *representatives* for our class? (pred. nominative)

6.   The children eagerly bought carnival *tickets*. (direct object)

7.   Her mother baked the *team* delicious brownies. (indirect object)

8.   You will soon become very *sleepy*. (pred. adjective)

9.   The angry man could not control his *temper*. (direct object)

10.   The cashier brought *Tim* a free soda. (indirect object)

Quiz #15

1.   She bought several *books* at the book fair. (direct object)

2.   My sister has become a very good soccer *player*. (pred. nominative)

3.   The pitcher threw the *catcher* an extremely fast pitch. (indirect object)

4.   No one seemed *excited* about the show. (pred. adjective)

5. The whole team was *exhausted* after the overnight trip. (pred. adjective)

6. She wrote her *name* carefully on the board. (direct object)

7. They ordered the debate *team* new membership pins. (indirect object)

8. My company will be the *sponsor* for the event. (pred. nominative)

9. We will be offering *support* for the auction. (direct object)

10. He has been my *friend* since third grade. (pred. nominative)

Chapter 4: Types of Nouns

In the following quizzes, students will be asked to identify a given noun as either *abstract*, *collective*, *common*, or *proper*. Collective nouns are not plurals, but singular nouns that represent more than one entity; abstract nouns are ideas that can have different interpretations for each individual; proper nouns are always capitalized; common nouns are everything else.

Students will write either <u>abstract</u> (abs.), <u>collective</u> (coll.), <u>common</u> (com.) or <u>proper</u> (prop.) on their papers. Answers are in parentheses.

Quiz #1

1.	flock	(collective)
2.	bikes	(common)
3.	sadness	(abstract)
4.	courage	(abstract)
5.	Washington Monument	(proper)
6.	band	(collective)
7.	leaves	(common)
8.	Yosemite National Park	(proper)
9.	concentration	(abstract)
10.	team	(collective)

Quiz #2

1.	flowers	(common)
2.	New York	(proper)

3.	troop	(collective)
4.	water	(common)
5.	joy	(abstract)
6.	shirt	(common)
7.	herd	(collective)
8.	girls	(common)
9.	band	(collective)
10.	sympathy	(abstract)

Quiz #3

1.	squad	(collective)
2.	freedom	(abstract)
3.	Madison Avenue	(proper)
4.	table	(common)
5.	committee	(collective)
6.	Friday	(proper)
7.	astonishment	(abstract)
8.	army	(collective)
9.	Lincoln Elementary School	(proper)
10.	fear	(abstract)

Quiz #4

1.	swarm	(collective)
2.	patriotism	(abstract)
3.	desks	(common)
4.	Washington, D.C.	(proper)

5.	kindness	(abstract)
6.	pictures	(common)
7.	jury	(collective)
8.	collection	(collective)
9.	sidewalk	(common)
10.	Maple Avenue	(proper)

Quiz #5

1.	council	(collective)
2.	politeness	(abstract)
3.	love	(abstract)
4.	bicycles	(common)
5.	San Francisco	(proper)
6.	choir	(collective)
7.	table	(common)
8.	determination	(abstract)
9.	bouquet	(collective)
10.	Indians	(proper)

Quiz #6

1.	door	(common)
2.	Black Beauty	(proper)
3.	anxiety	(abstract)
4.	rug	(common)
5.	committee	(collective)
6.	Carson City	(proper)

7.	loyalty	(abstract)
8.	gathering	(collective)
9.	puppies	(common)
10.	security	(abstract)

Quiz #7

1.	hatred	(abstract)
2.	Pacific Ocean	(proper)
3.	monkey	(common)
4.	concentration	(abstract)
5.	Pepsi	(proper)
6.	garden	(collective)
7.	telephone	(common)
8.	courtesy	(abstract)
9.	crew	(collective)
10.	American	(proper)

Quiz #8

1.	tray	(common)
2.	forest	(collective)
3.	Mr. Adams	(proper)
4.	Saturday	(proper)
5.	dream	(abstract)
6.	sofa	(common)
7.	bunch	(collective)
8.	majesty	(abstract)

| 9. | herd | (collective) |
| 10. | glasses | (common) |

Quiz #9

1.	pencil	(common)
2.	Mt. Rushmore	(proper)
3.	Dr. Morgan	(proper)
4.	independence	(abstract)
5.	association	(collective)
6.	basketball	(common)
7.	skill	(abstract)
8.	fans	(common)
9.	organization	(collective)
10.	Lake Erie	(proper)

Quiz #10

1.	Dodge Ram	(proper)
2.	band	(collective)
3.	car	(common)
4.	kindness	(abstract)
5.	Lincoln Elementary	(proper)
6.	gang	(collective)
7.	comedy	(abstract)
8.	boat	(common)
9.	Mississippi River	(proper)
10.	fear	(abstract)

Chapter 5: Plural Nouns

The quizzes in this section will deal with the formation of nouns in plurals. Most nouns in the English language form their plurals by adding "s." There are basic rules that govern the plural formation of other nouns. Some of those rules and a few examples follow.

There are some words whose form does not change when they become plural (*sheep, sheep; deer, deer; moose, moose*). Certain words change their spelling completely (*child, children; ox, oxen; mouse, mice; tooth, teeth*). Most words ending in "s," "x," "ch," and "sh" form their plurals by adding "es" (*glass, glasses; church, churches; box, boxes; dish, dishes*). Spelling of these plurals is easy if students listen to the way the words are pronounced. If there is a "y" at the end of the word with a consonant in front of it, the plural is formed by changing the "y" to "i" and adding "es" (*family, families; county, counties; penny, pennies*). If there is a vowel before the "y," the plural is formed by simply adding an "s" (*monkey, monkeys; boy, boys; play, plays*). The plural formation of words ending in "o" and "fe" or "f" has no set rule. Words ending in "o" can be spelled with just an "s" or an "es." Generally, words ending in "o" that have to do with music, only add an "s" to form their plurals (*piano, pianos, solo, solos*). Words ending in "fe" or "f" are made plural by adding an "s" or by changing the "f" to "v" and adding "es." They just have to be learned, practiced, and remembered.

Students will be given a word, and they must write the plural form of that word. Regular words that form their plurals with "s" will not be included. Answers will be shown in parentheses.

Quiz #1

1. child (children)
2. ox (oxen)
3. box (boxes)
4. monkey (monkeys)
5. church (churches)
6. moose (moose)
7. family (families)
8. tooth (teeth)
9. dish (dishes)
10. hero (heroes)

Quiz #2

1. sheep (sheep)
2. ax (axes)
3. stereo (stereos)
4. soprano (sopranos)
5. turkey (turkeys)
6. echo (echoes)
7. chief (chiefs)
8. country (countries)
9. brush (brushes)
10. man (men)

Quiz #3

1. potato (potatoes)

2.	knife	(knives)
3.	class	(classes)
4.	baby	(babies)
5.	goose	(geese)
6.	child	(children)
7.	valley	(valleys)
8.	roof	(roofs)
9.	radio	(radios)
10.	deer	(deer)

Quiz #4

1.	wife	(wives)
2.	piano	(pianos)
3.	bench	(benches)
4.	lady	(ladies)
5.	hoof	(hooves)
6.	salmon	(salmon)
7.	donkey	(donkeys)
8.	hero	(heroes)
9.	chairman	(chairmen)
10.	dress	(dresses)

Quiz #5

1.	tuna	(tuna)
2.	veto	(vetoes)
3.	woman	(women)

4.	bay	(bays)
5.	wish	(wishes)
6.	mouse	(mice)
7.	solo	(solos)
8.	enemy	(enemies)
9.	beach	(beaches)
10.	shelf	(shelves)

Quiz #6

1.	auto	(autos)
2.	elk	(elk)
3.	wolf	(wolves)
4.	tomato	(tomatoes)
5.	city	(cities)
6.	chief	(chiefs)
7.	tray	(trays)
8.	patch	(patches)
9.	fox	(foxes)
10.	princess	(princesses)

Quiz #7

1.	company	(companies)
2.	calf	(calves)
3.	ditch	(ditches)
4.	moose	(moose)
5.	cargo	(cargoes)

6.	relay	(relays)
7.	radish	(radishes)
8.	ox	(oxen)
9.	library	(libraries)
10.	studio	(studios)

Quiz #8

1.	trout	(trout)
2.	alley	(alleys)
3.	sketch	(sketches)
4.	brief	(briefs)
5.	leaf	(leaves)
6.	lobby	(lobbies)
7.	business	(businesses)
8.	tooth	(teeth)
9.	sheep	(sheep)
10.	potato	(potatoes)

Quiz #9

1.	half	(halves)
2.	radio	(radios)
3.	key	(keys)
4.	lunch	(lunches)
5.	octopus	(octopi)
6.	belief	(beliefs)
7.	foot	(feet)

8.	deer	(deer)
9.	veto	(vetoes)
10.	rally	(rallies)

Quiz #10

1.	lily	(lilies)
2.	boy	(boys)
3.	loss	(losses)
4.	dish	(dishes)
5.	chef	(chefs)
6.	duo	(duos)
7.	echo	(echoes)
8.	elf	(elves)
9.	birch	(birches)
10.	woman	(women)

Chapter 6: Possessive Nouns

The nouns in this section will show ownership. There are three very simple rules that govern the spelling of possessives, all of which must include an *apostrophe*.

➤ Any <u>singular</u> noun, regardless of the letter at its end, will form its possessive by adding "'s."

➤ Any <u>plural</u> noun that ends in "s" will form its possessive simply by adding an apostrophe.

➤ Any <u>plural</u> noun that does not end in an "s" forms its possessive by adding 's, just like a singular noun. These rules will govern <u>every</u> case of ownership or possession.

In the following quizzes there will be words, followed by a "one" or a "more" in parentheses (to designate singular or plural), and then the answer in parentheses. Students will write the correct spelling with the proper placement of the apostrophe in each.

Quiz #1

1.	business	(more)	(businesses')
2.	sky	(one)	(sky's)
3.	man	(more)	(men's)
4.	waitress	(one)	(waitress's)
5.	Chris	(one)	(Chris's)
6.	student	(more)	(students')
7.	baby	(more)	(babies')
8.	sheep	(more)	(sheep's)
9.	box	(more)	(boxes')

| 10. | goose | (one) | (goose's) |

Quiz #2

1.	princess	(one)	(princess's)
2.	child	(more)	(children's)
3.	car	(more)	(cars')
4.	friend	(one)	(friend's)
5.	dress	(more)	(dresses')
6.	tooth	(more)	(teeth's)
7.	valley	(one)	(valley's)
8.	tree	(more)	(trees')
9.	teacher	(more)	(teachers')
10.	Jess	(one)	(Jess's)

Quiz #3

1.	dog	(more)	(dogs')
2.	man	(more)	(men's)
3.	address	(one)	(address's)
4.	doctor	(more)	(doctors')
5.	lady	(one)	(lady's)
6.	church	(more)	(churches')
7.	deer	(more)	(deer's)
8.	Jonas	(one)	(Jonas's)
9.	bike	(more)	(bikes')
10.	wolf	(more)	(wolves')

Quiz #4

1.	Francis	(one)		(Francis's)
2.	school	(more)		(schools')
3.	salmon	(more)		(salmon's)
4.	truck	(one)		(truck's)
5.	witness	(more)		(witnesses')
6.	door	(one)		(door's)
7.	musician	(more)		(musicians')
8.	student	(more)		(students')
9.	county	(one)		(county's)
10.	actress	(one)		(actress's)

Quiz #5

1.	man	(one)		(man's)
2.	window	(more)		(windows')
3.	daisy	(more)		(daisies')
4.	door	(one)		(door's)
5.	business	(one)		(business's)
6.	train	(more)		(trains')
7.	mouse	(one)		(mouse's)
8.	church	(more)		(churches')
9.	calf	(more)		(calves')
10.	camera	(one)		(camera's)

Quiz #6

1.	fox	(more)		(foxes')

77

2.	woman	(more)	(women's)
3.	tree	(one)	(tree's)
4.	moose	(more)	(moose's)
5.	actress	(one)	(actress's)
6.	roof	(more)	(roofs')
7.	monkey	(more)	(monkeys')
8.	city	(one)	(city's)
9.	deputy	(more)	(deputies')
10.	beach	(more)	(beaches')

Quiz #7

1.	hero	(more)	(heroes')
2.	book	(more)	(books')
3.	boy	(one)	(boy's)
4.	class	(one)	(class's)
5.	party	(more)	(parties')
6.	wall	(one)	(wall's)
7.	lady	(one)	(lady's)
8.	piano	(more)	(pianos')
9.	waitress	(more)	(waitresses')
10.	ox	(more)	(oxen's)

Quiz #8

1.	auto	(more)	(autos')
2.	child	(more)	(children's)
3.	dress	(one)	(dress's)

4.	baby	(more)	(babies')
5.	bus	(one)	(bus's)
6.	county	(one)	(county's)
7.	hostess	(more)	(hostesses')
8.	goose	(one)	(goose's)
9.	mouse	(more)	(mice's)
10.	family	(one)	(family's)

Quiz #9

1.	salmon	(more)	(salmon's)
2.	dress	(one)	(dress's)
3.	jury	(more)	(juries')
4.	James	(one)	(James's)
5.	tomato	(more)	(tomatoes')
6.	knife	(more)	(knives')
7.	country	(one)	(country's)
8.	rocket	(more)	(rockets')
9.	earmuff	(one)	(earmuff's)
10.	goose	(more)	(geese's)

Quiz #10

1.	glass	(one)	(glass's)
2.	parent	(more)	(parents')
3.	Lucas	(one)	(Lucas's)
4.	toy	(more)	(toys')
5.	dish	(more)	(dishes')

6.	porch	(one)	(porch's)
7.	state	(one)	(state's)
8.	stereo	(more)	(stereos')
9.	berry	(more)	(berries')
10.	bluff	(one)	(bluff's)

Quiz #11

1.	Jones	(more)	(Joneses')
2.	road	(one)	(road's)
3.	lunch	(more)	(lunches')
4.	tray	(more)	(trays')
5.	memo	(one)	(memo's)
6.	lash	(more)	(lashes')
7.	picture	(one)	(picture's)
8.	memory	(more)	(memories')
9.	freshman	(more)	(freshmen's)
10.	shelf	(one)	(shelf's)

Quiz #12

1.	mouse	(more)	(mice's)
2.	bowl	(one)	(bowl's)
3.	ax	(more)	(axes')
4.	punch	(one)	(punch's)
5.	dress	(more)	(dresses')
6.	woman	(more)	(women's)
7.	fence	(one)	(fence's)

8.	chief	(more)	(chiefs')
9.	leaf	(more)	(leaves')
10.	lady	(more)	(ladies')

Quiz #13

1.	speech	(one)	(speech's)
2.	puppy	(more)	(puppies')
3.	bush	(more)	(bushes')
4.	necklace	(one)	(necklace's)
5.	Las Vegas	(one)	(Las Vegas's)
6.	wall	(more)	(walls')
7.	play	(more)	(plays')
8.	address	(more)	(addresses')
9.	peak	(one)	(peak's)
10.	photo	(more)	(photos')

Quiz #14

1.	halo	(more)	(halos')
2.	sweater	(one)	(sweater's)
3.	echo	(more)	(echoes')
4.	hoof	(more)	(hooves')
5.	bell	(one)	(bell's)
6.	child	(more)	(children's)
7.	wish	(more)	(wishes')
8.	Friday	(one)	(Friday's)
9.	ox	(more)	(oxen's)

10.   wristwatch   (one)   (wristwatch's)

Quiz #15

1.   path   (one)   (path's)
2.   elf   (more)   (elves')
3.   turkey   (more)   (turkeys')
4.   fish   (one)   (fish's)
5.   torch   (more)   (torches')
6.   compass   (one)   (compass's)
7.   lake   (more)   (lakes')
8.   pencil   (one)   (pencil's)
9.   lobby   (more)   (lobbies')
10. veto   (more)   (vetoes')

Section II: PRONOUNS

Chapter 7: Number and Person

The quizzes in this section will review one of the most difficult parts of speech, pronouns. The difficulty lies not in the recognition of pronouns, but in the agreement of pronouns, (especially indefinite pronouns), with the verb, in choosing the correct indefinite pronoun, and the correct pronoun form in compounds.

In the first section, each quiz will consist of ten questions requiring the student to identify the person, number, and type of pronoun. These quizzes should be given after students are familiar with the personal pronoun chart. Quizzes should be read giving the person first (1, 2, or 3), the number second (singular or plural), and the type third. Students will write the correct pronoun only. Answers will be in parentheses at the end of each formula.

Quiz #1

1.	1p	singular	pronominal adj.	(my)
2.	3p	plural	subject	(they)
3.	1p	plural	object	(us)
4.	3p	singular	possessive (masc.)	(his)
5.	2p	singular	object	(you)
6.	1p	singular	reflexive	(myself)
7.	3p	singular	subject (fem.)	(she)
8.	2p	plural	subject	(you)
9.	1p	plural	pronominal adj.	(our)
10.	3p	plural	reflexive	(themselves)

Quiz #2

1.	1p	plural	subject	(we)
2.	3p	singular	reflexive (fem.)	(herself)
3.	2p	singular	pronominal adj.	(your)
4.	1p	singular	possessive	(mine)
5.	3p	plural	object	(them)
6.	3p	singular	pronominal adj. (neuter)	(its)
7.	2p	plural	reflexive	(yourselves)
8.	1p	plural	object	(us)
9.	3p	plural	possessive	(theirs)
10.	1p	plural	reflexive	(ourselves)

Quiz #3

1.	2p	plural	reflexive	(yourselves)
2.	1p	singular	possessive	(mine)
3.	3p	singular	pronominal adj. (masc.)	(his)
4.	1p	plural	object	(us)
5.	2p	plural	possessive	(yours)
6.	3p	singular	subject (fem.)	(she)
7.	1p	singular	reflexive	(myself)
8.	3p	plural	object	(them)
9.	1p	singular	pronominal adj.	(my)
10.	3p	singular	possessive (neuter)	(its)

Quiz #4

1.	1p	singular	subject	(I)

86

2.	3p	plural	object	(them)
3.	2p	singular	reflexive	(yourself)
4.	1p	plural	pronominal adj.	(our)
5.	3p	singular	possessive (neuter)	(its)
6.	1p	singular	possessive	(mine)
7.	3p	singular	reflexive (masc.)	(himself)
8.	2p	plural	possessive	(yours)
9.	3p	plural	pronominal adj.	(their)
10.	3p	singular	subject (fem.)	(she)

Quiz #5

1.	1p	singular	pronominal adj.	(my)
2.	2p	plural	possessive	(yours)
3.	2p	singular	subject	(you)
4.	3p	singular	possessive (neuter)	(its)
5.	3p	plural	reflexive	(themselves)
6.	1p	singular	subject	(I)
7.	1p	plural	possessive	(ours)
8.	3p	singular	possessive (masc.)	(his)
9.	3p	plural	pronominal adj.	(their)
10.	2p	singular	reflexive	(yourself)

Quiz #6

1.	1p	plural	possessive	(ours)
2.	3p	singular	subject (masc.)	(he)
3.	2p	plural	object	(you)

4.	1p	singular	object	(me)
5.	3p	plural	subject	(they)
6.	2p	singular	pronominal adj.	(your)
7.	3p	plural	object	(them)
8.	1p	singular	possessive	(mine)
9.	3p	plural	reflexive	(themselves)
10.	2p	singular	possessive	(yours)

Quiz #7

1.	3p	singular	pronominal adj. (fem.)	(her)
2.	1p	singular	subject	(I)
3.	2p	singular	reflexive	(yourself)
4.	1p	plural	pronominal adj.	(our)
5.	3p	singular	possessive (neuter)	(its)
6.	2p	plural	possessive	(yours)
7.	3p	singular	pronominal adj. (masc.)	(his)
8.	2p	singular	subject	(you)
9.	1p	plural	reflexive	(ourselves)
10.	3p	singular	object (neuter)	(it)

Quiz #8

1.	3p	plural	subject	(they)
2.	1p	plural	object	(us)
3.	3p	plural	reflexive	(themselves)
4.	1p	singular	pronominal adj.	(my)
5.	2p	plural	reflexive	(yourselves)

6.	3p	singular	object (masc.)	(him)
7.	3p	singular	subject (fem.)	(she)
8.	2p	plural	subject	(you)
9.	3p	plural	pronominal adj.	(their)
10.	1p	singular	reflexive	(myself)

Quiz #9

1.	1p	plural	pronominal adj.	(our)
2.	3p	plural	possessive	(theirs)
3.	1p	singular	object	(me)
4.	3p	singular	object (fem.)	(her)
5.	3p	singular	pronominal adj. (neuter)	(its)
6.	1p	plural	reflexive	(ourselves)
7.	2p	plural	pronominal adj.	(your)
8.	1p	plural	subject	(we)
9.	3p	singular	possessive (fem.)	(hers)
10.	3p	singular	reflexive (masc.)	(himself)

Quiz #10

1.	1p	singular	possessive	(mine)
2.	3p	singular	subject (fem.)	(she)
3.	1p	plural	subject	(we)
4.	3p	plural	reflexive	(yourselves)
5.	1p	plural	possessive	(ours)
6.	3p	singular	pronominal adj. (masc.)	(his)
7.	1p	plural	object	(us)

8.	3p	singular	reflexive (fem.)	(herself)
9.	2p	singular	subject	(you)
10.	3p	plural	object	(them)

Chapter 8: Recognizing All Pronouns

In the following quizzes, students will be asked to identify all pronouns in each sentence. As in the noun section, a number in parentheses at the end of each sentence tells how many pronouns it contains to aid in recognition if necessary, and each pronoun is identified by italics. The section will include subject, object, possessive, reflexive, interrogative, demonstrative, and indefinite pronouns as well as pronominal adjectives.

Quiz #1

1. *He* quickly ran toward *them*, and *everyone* cheered. (3)

2. *Each* of the boys brought *his* with *him* to class. (3)

3. *She* and *I* will go with *her* to the movies. (3)

4. *That* will cause many problems for *me*. (2)

5. *Nobody* could hear *us* when the bell was ringing. (2)

6. *Nothing* will stop *her* from doing a good job on *her* presentation. (3)

7. *Those* will help *you* remember where to drop *them* off. (3)

8. *None* of *us* could remember *his* name. (3)

9. *Either* of the groups would do a good job for *him* and *her*. (3)

10. *This* is the end of the road, and *I* don't see *her* anywhere. (3)

Quiz #2

1.   That boy said *that* to *me* and *my* friend. (3)

2.   *All* of *us* will go with *them* to see *her*. (4)

3.   *You* should go with *him* to see *their* performance. (3)

4.   *Nobody* wanted *this* so *we* voted against *it*.   (4)

5.   *Either* of *her* plans would have given *him* an advantage. (3)

6.   *Those* will have to entertain *them* until *we* can get *more*. (4)

7.   *Each* of *them* has selected a place for *you* to visit. (3)

8.   *Some* of *it* was not eaten at *their* party. (3)

9.   *Everyone* wanted *her* to win, but *she* did not. (3)

10.   *My* mom and *I* went with *him* to pick *it* up. (4)

Quiz #3

1.   *Both* of *us* will be returning with *her*.   (3)

2.   *Theirs* was better than *ours*. (2)

3.   *She* and *I* will run get *them* for *everyone*. (4)

4.   *Her* bicycle was parked by *mine* and *his*. (3)

5.   *Those* belong to *her* brother and *me*. (3)

6.   *Nothing* was wrong with *it* as far as *we* could see. (3)

7.   *Everything they* brought was sold by *us*. (3)

8.   *Neither* of the jobs was the right choice for *him* or *her*. (3)

9.   *He* and *she* will bring *them* to *your* house for *him*. (5)

10. *Your* mother gave *me this* to give to *you*. (4)

Quiz #4

1. *Each* of *them* brought *his* project to *her*. (4)

2. *Several* of the girls decided to wear *that*. (2)

3. *Nothing* could prevent *him* from going with *her*. (3)

4. *Mine* was on that shelf beside *hers*. (2)

5. *She* and *I* will challenge *you* to a final race. (3)

6. *Neither* of *us* could believe *she* had come with *them*. (4)

7. *Some* of *you* can combine *yours* with *theirs*. (4)

8. *Everyone* could hear *it*. (2)

9. *This* is *her* project, but *I* want to show *you ours*. (5)

10. *You* and *I* should go with *them* to *that*. (4)

Quiz #5

1. *Someone* should run with *him* to get *it*. (3)

2. *She* and *I* bought *that* for *her*. (4)

3. *Everything* on that table belongs to *somebody*. (2)

4. *We* said *they* only wanted *some* of *them*. (4)

5. *Either* of the girls could have brought *it*. (2)

6. *Those* on the field belong to *our* school and *his*. (3)

7. Are *you* coming with *us* tonight to meet *everyone* at *my* house? (4)

8. *Nothing* could be done about *our* small problem. (2)

9. *Her* art display will be at *their* gallery. (2)

10. *He* and *my* brother returned *their* rented equipment to the shop. (3)

Quiz #6

1. *He* and *she* brought *everything* with *them*. (4)

2. *Many* of *us* have *nothing* formal to wear. (3)

3. *His* friend sent *several* of *them* to *us*. (4)

4. *This* in *my* hand is *hers*. (3)

5. *Those who* were at the party saw *us*. (3)

6. *Your* table looks beautiful, and *we* are excited to be at *your* house. (3)

7. *I* saw *her* with *someone* near *their* shop. (4)

8. *Which* did *she* bring with *her* last night? (3)

9. *Someone* sent *him* to get *it* from *us*. (4)

10. *Whom* did *they* select for *her* assistant? (3)

Quiz #7

1. *No one* saw *him* without *it*. (3)

2. *That* is the book *I* borrowed from *her* after school. (3)

3. *Everything* on the living room table was *hers*. (2)

4. *Whom they* would select was the question. (2)

5. *He* and *my* father took *those* with *them*. (4)

6. *Each* of *her* brothers is playing *his* guitar in *our* program. (4)

7. *Her* friends told *each* of *them* about *it*. (4)

8. *She* and *I* arrived there with *all* of *our* luggage. (4)

9. *Somebody* saw *them* on the street by *their* house. (3)

10. *My* youngest sister told *everybody* *her* deepest secrets. (3)

Quiz #8

1. *Others* found *their* way to the park. (2)

2. *Whom* are *they* going to find as *her* replacement? (3)

3. *These* are not the *same* as *those*. (3)

4. *His* face was recognizable to *everyone* in the room. (2)

5. *Neither* of *us* is the person for *whom* *you* are looking. (4)

6. *This* is *my* neighbor's, and *mine* is over there. (3)

7. *Someone* left *it* on *my* doorstep, and *I* found *it* this morning. (5)

8. *What* is the answer to *her* question and *mine*? (3)

9. *Much* of the time *she* is at *his* house with *others*. (4)

10. *Your* grandparents sent *them* gifts from *their* vacation. (3)

Quiz #9

1. *Many* of the students had left *them* in *their* rooms. (3)

2. *Who* will be the speaker at *our* next meeting after *this*? (3)

3. The three of *us* had asked *everyone* to bring *anything* *they* could find. (4)

4.   *This* is the last roll of trash bags in *his* garage. (2)

5.   There were *others who* noticed *her* near the river with *her* brother. (4)

6.   *I* cannot remember *whom we* selected to lead that committee. (3)

7.   Susan saw *both* of *those* on *her* brief tour of the museum. (3)

8.   *She* and *I* are already at the theater with the *others*. (3)

9.   Fred and *she* took *their* special trip after seeing *his* and *her* pictures. (4)

10. *Which* did *he* decide to change on the last page of *their* test? (3)

Quiz #10

1.   *No one* saw *them* after *it* was over, and *everybody* had left. (4)

2.   The people in line were waiting for *their* tickets to *it*. (2)

3.   *Someone* must be wondering *whom they* selected for *that*. (4)

4.   The end of the line came more quickly than *he* and *she* knew. (2)

5.   *My* friend took the pie to *her* house before *they* arrived. (3)

6.   Without the *others nobody* could remember *who* was in charge. (3)

7.   Shawn and *his* brother brought *several* with *them* to the event. (3)

8. The college accepted *her* brother and *your* sister for *their* event. (3)

9. *Everybody* wants *his* own room on *our* summer trip. (3)

10. Without *her* and *you, nothing* on that list makes sense. (3)

Chapter 9: Subject and Object Pronouns

Correct usage of subject and object pronouns has become increasingly difficult over the years, especially when used in a compound structure. There is a simple solution to this problem if students drop the compound part of the sentence and use each pronoun by itself. Seldom will a mistake be made this way. It is just a matter of being willing to slow down and take the time to find the correct answer. The more students practice with this method, the less it becomes necessary. Subject pronouns must be used as subjects and predicate nominatives. Object pronouns must be used as direct objects, indirect objects, and objects of the preposition. When deciding between *who* (subject) and *whom* (object), it is only necessary to replace *who* with *he* and *whom* with *him* to find the correct answer. *Whom* is always used with a preposition in a sentence without clauses.

In these quizzes there will be ten sentences, each with a choice of two pronouns in parentheses. Students will write the proper choice. The correct answer will be underlined. Reminders about removing the compound part will prove helpful.

Quiz #1

1. That boy and (<u>I</u>, me) will be the first in line.

2. The person on the phone was (<u>she</u>, her).

3. Please return the magazines to (she, <u>her</u>).

4. They received a beautiful gift from her cousin and (I, <u>me</u>).

5. He carried the groceries in for (we, <u>us</u>).

6. The superintendent and (<u>he</u>, him) could not find the water leak.

7. Tom and (<u>he</u>, him) were invited to come along with us.

8. He bought cookies for his coach and (we, <u>us</u>).

9. Tomorrow night the team and (<u>I</u>, me) will finish the posters.

10. Will you please talk to (she, <u>her</u>)?

Quiz #2

1. The winner of that last event was (<u>he</u>, him).

2. My friends and (<u>I</u>, me) will be going to the mall on Saturday.

3. Will you please send the information to Frank and (we, <u>us</u>)?

4. Another letter has arrived from (they, <u>them</u>).

5. Between Theresa and (I, <u>me</u>), we now have fifteen entries.

6. The owners and (<u>she</u>, her) have finally agreed on a date for the event.

7. In the morning my youngest brother and (<u>he</u>, him) will be leaving for camp.

8. The presents were all bought by (we, <u>us</u>).

9. The final contestant should have been (<u>she</u>, her).

10. (<u>He</u>, Him) and my mother will arrive home shortly.

Quiz #3

1. Please give the questions to Sam and (he, <u>him</u>).

2. (<u>She</u>, Her) and my brother went to the movie at the mall.

3. (Who, <u>Whom</u>) did they select as chairman of the committee?

4. My friend and (<u>I</u>, me) saw two movies last weekend.

5. We received a letter from Sue and (he, <u>him</u>).

6. The person on the phone was (<u>I</u>, me).

7. (<u>Who</u>, Whom) will be the overall winner?

8. He mailed a large package to my sister and (we, <u>us</u>).

9. The biggest jackpot winner was (<u>she</u>, her).

10. (<u>They</u>, Them) and the parents left later that afternoon.

Quiz #4

1. With (who, <u>whom</u>) will you be traveling?

2. My friends and (<u>I</u>, me) are going to the basketball game.

3. The person on the stage is (<u>he</u>, him).

4. We bought several gifts for my cousins and (they, <u>them</u>).

5. Her brother and (<u>she</u>, her) will come by the house later.

6. Your best friend is (<u>who</u>, whom)?

7. Her coach sent a letter to her parents and (she, <u>her</u>).

8. Her new lab partners will be (<u>they</u>, them).

9. The other contestants and (<u>we</u>, us) toured the entire city.

10. (Who, <u>Whom</u>) did you call for a ride?

Quiz #5

1.   A postcard arrived from my brother and (he, <u>him</u>).

2.   From (who, <u>whom</u>) did you receive that sweater?

3.   My new partner for the race was (<u>she</u>, her).

4.   Another student and (<u>I</u>, me) heard the strange noise first.

5.   Please take this stack of papers from (we, <u>us</u>).

6.   (<u>She</u>, Her) and Jim will be leaving for the game soon.

7.   Between her instructor and (they, <u>them</u>,) an argument is always brewing.

8.   (<u>Who</u>, Whom) will be running the next relay?

9.   The person in the contest last year was (<u>I</u>, me).

10. Near Sue and (he, <u>him</u>) stood a very high brick wall.

Quiz #6

1.   My mom and (<u>I</u>, me) will be going to the market on Saturday.

2.   The others in the group and (<u>we</u>, us) would like a chance at a rematch.

3.   I sent an invitation to John and (he, <u>him</u>).

4.   The girl who won the prize was (<u>she</u>, her).

5.   The large dog started moving toward my brother and (she, <u>her</u>).

6.   My sister brought Sue and (I, <u>me</u>) an ice cream cake.

7.   We bought all of our books from that man and (they, <u>them</u>).

8.   My brother and (<u>she</u>, her) will be going with us.

9.   They took all of the paper away from Frank and (she, <u>her</u>).

10.   The champion of the day for that event was (<u>I</u>, me).

Quiz #7

1.   To (who, <u>whom</u>) did you give the package?

2.   Everyone wanted to go along with Frank and (he, <u>him</u>).

3.   The best speaker at the event was (<u>she</u>, her).

4.   (Who, <u>Whom</u>) do you want on your team?

5.   My dad and (<u>I</u>, me) went to the store very early.

6.   To Sharon and (they, <u>them</u>), we sent cards.

7.   I received a beautiful bouquet from Susan and (she, <u>her</u>).

8.   (<u>They</u>, Them) and my other friends stopped at our game.

9.   (<u>Who</u>, Whom) will be picking me up from school?

10.   The person on the phone could have been (<u>he</u>, him).

Quiz #8

1.   My mother and (<u>I</u>, me) will be at the mall by 3 o'clock to meet you.

2.   The realtor looked for an apartment for her sister and (she, <u>her</u>).

3.   For (who, <u>whom</u>) was that large package delivered?

4.   The new employee of the month is (<u>he</u>, him).

5.   There was definitely an agreement between my aunt and (they, <u>them</u>).

6. You and (<u>she</u>, her) are the next two in line.

7. (<u>Who</u>, Whom) is the person on the other end of the line?

8. Fred and (<u>they</u>, them) are coming to the party a little later.

9. The people at the store gave a candy sample to my friend and (I, <u>me</u>).

10. If you hear a very hoarse voice, it is (<u>I</u>, me).

Quiz #9

1. (Who, <u>Whom</u>) are you inviting to the prom on Saturday?

2. Her brother and (<u>he</u>, him) are leaving soon for a trip to Europe.

3. The concert program was given to Frank and (she, <u>her</u>).

4. Her boss and (<u>they</u>, them) planned the entire conference themselves.

5. The small dog and (<u>I</u>, me) took a long walk around the park.

6. We were asked to sit between Steve and (she, <u>her</u>).

7. He was the person (<u>who</u>, whom) was asked the last question.

8. (<u>She</u>, Her) and her friends stopped by for a swim.

9. That woman and (<u>I</u>, me) will be going on stage together.

10. The next person on his list was (<u>I</u>, me).

Quiz #10

1. My best friend at school is (<u>she</u>, her).

2. (<u>Who</u>, Whom) will bring the others to the game?

3. We created a beautiful event for the company and (they, <u>them</u>).

4. The old man and (<u>he</u>, him) left the hospital together.

5. (<u>She</u>, Her) and my sister have always been very competitive.

6. (Who, <u>Whom</u>) did the candidate select as a running mate.

7. The person on the phone was (<u>I</u>, me).

8. Nothing had been resolved between the company and (she, <u>her</u>).

9. (<u>He</u>, Him) and I will be home right after school.

10. To (who, <u>whom</u>) did the college mail the letter?

Chapter 10: Combined Pronoun Practice

The quizzes in this section will offer a variety of challenges, including indefinite pronoun subject/verb agreement and proper pronominal adjective usage. It will also continue the review of proper subject/object pronoun use. There will be ten questions in each section, and the answers will be underlined from a choice of two words in parentheses.

Remember: Any indefinite pronoun ending in *-one, -body,* or *-thing* is singular, as are *neither, either, each,* and *much*.

Determining which verb to use for singular is confusing for students as well since *I* cannot determine a singular verb. Instead, students should use *he* to find a singular verb and *they* to find a plural verb. Many of the correct pronouns will sound wrong since few people use indefinite pronouns properly.

Students will write the correct choice from the words in parentheses.

Quiz #1

1. Everyone needed (<u>his</u>, their) own supplies.

2. Our whole club was seated between Ellie and (I, <u>me</u>).

3. Neither of the members (<u>has</u>, have) the new schedule.

4. The last person on the talk show was (<u>she</u>, her).

5. Each of the students has (<u>his</u>, their) own locker.

6. We quickly addressed the letter to (he, <u>him</u>).

7. A late package arrived from my aunt and (she, <u>her</u>).

8. Either of the rooms (<u>is</u>, are) acceptable.

9. The guest at the end of the table was (<u>I</u>, me).

10. (<u>She</u>, Her) and my best friend are visiting me this weekend.

Quiz #2

1. Everybody needs to practice (<u>his</u>, their) lines.

2. My mom and (<u>she</u>, her) will be picking us up in an hour.

3. We wanted to give a party for Hank and (she, <u>her</u>).

4. Each of the candidates (<u>wants</u>, want) more airtime.

5. To (who, <u>whom</u>) did she speak on the phone.

6. (Who, <u>Whom</u>) will the club choose as president?

7. Neither of the boys (<u>remembers</u>, remember) the way to the field.

8. No one chose (<u>his</u>, their) elective until today.

9. Both of the boys (plays, <u>play</u>) baseball well.

10. My partner for the event will be (<u>he</u>, him).

Quiz #3

1. Everyone needs to bring (<u>his</u>, their) calculator to math.

2. Neither of the members (<u>wants</u>, want) to be the chairman.

3. My father and (<u>I</u>, me) will be studying science tonight.

4. Several of the numbers (was, <u>were</u>) missing from the stack.

5. Each of the players (<u>passes</u>, pass) the ball very well.

6. My best friend on the whole trip was (<u>she</u>, her).

7. She brought sandwiches to the players and (they, <u>them</u>).

8. With (who, <u>whom</u>) will she be going on vacation?

9. No one could remember (<u>his</u>, their) lines for the play.

10. (Who, <u>Whom</u>) did they choose to lead the discussion?

Quiz #4

1. (<u>Who</u>, Whom) will be the next contestant?

2. My brother and (<u>she</u>, her) were the first in line for tickets.

3. Neither of the best prizes (<u>was</u>, were) won.

4. Everyone needs to remove (<u>his</u>, their) supplies from the closet.

5. By (who, <u>whom</u>) were you trained?

6. The winner of the very best prize was (<u>he</u>, him).

7. Each of the bottles (<u>contains</u>, contain) the same soda.

8. From my mother and (he, <u>him</u>), I received a new watch.

9. No one in my group had brought (<u>his</u>, their) books.

10. My sister wants to sit between you and (I, <u>me</u>).

Quiz #5

1. Each of the players (<u>needs</u>, need) a new jersey.

2. To (who, <u>whom</u>) did you send the request?

3. Frank and (<u>he</u>, him) will be selecting the teams.

4. Neither of my friends brought (<u>his</u>, their) tennis racket.

5. Can she give the prize to my brother and (I, <u>me</u>)?

6. (<u>We</u>, Us) girls will be in the next tournament.

7. The sponsor arranged for Sam and (they, <u>them</u>) to take a tour.

8. Someone has left (<u>her</u>, their) books on the locker.

9. My mother and (<u>she</u>, her) will pick me up in an hour.

10. Everyone wanted (<u>his</u>, their) own copy of the book.

Quiz #6

1. My mother and (<u>I</u>, me) went to the grocery store.

2. Each of the prizes (<u>was</u>, were) bought last week.

3. Please bring the books to Pat and (she, <u>her</u>).

4. Neither of the students brought (<u>his</u>, their) binders.

5. From Sally and (I, <u>me</u>) she received a wool scarf.

6. Everyone wanted to purchase (<u>his</u>, their) own plane ticket.

7. The Wilsons and (<u>she</u>, her) will arrive at 3 o'clock.

8. We will all go to the game with my father and (they, <u>them</u>).

9. Either of the coaches (<u>has</u>, have) the score.

10. All of the performances (was, <u>were</u>) rescheduled.

Quiz #7

1. Fred and (<u>she</u>, her) are coming with us to the game.

2. Everyone wants to carry (<u>his</u>, their) own luggage.

3. Please tell the story for Sheila and (I, <u>me</u>).

4. Neither of the glasses on the counter (<u>is</u>, are) clean.

5. The waiter brought Frank and (we, <u>us</u>) glasses of water.

6. Few of the prizes (is, <u>are</u>) left.

7. Each of the winners (<u>was</u>, were) given a prize.

8. The judges were willing to listen to (they, <u>them</u>).

9. She and (<u>I</u>, me) started for the mall early in the morning.

10. The secretary made an appointment for my mother and (she, <u>her</u>).

Quiz #8

1. No one remembered to bring (<u>his</u>, their) literature book to class.

2. In the morning my sister and (<u>I</u>, me) will be leaving on our trip.

3. (Who, <u>Whom</u>) did you call last night?

4. The goals were made by my brother and (she, <u>her</u>).

5. Everything in the bags (<u>has</u>, have) been distributed.

6. The main characters in the play were Sam and (<u>I</u>, me).

7. From (who, <u>whom</u>) did the letter come?

8. Some of the pie (<u>was</u>, were) eaten before dinner.

9.   My father and (<u>he</u>, him) planned the whole camping trip.

10.   They arranged the event for the other students and (he, <u>him</u>).

Quiz #9

1.   Several of the boys (was, <u>were</u>) waiting for the coach.

2.   The climbers on the top of the cliff were my best friend and (<u>he</u>, him).

3.   Each of the kittens had (<u>its</u>, their) own mouse.

4.   She and (<u>he</u>, him) will be the princess and prince of the prom.

5.   Either of the young men (<u>is</u>, are) acceptable for the job.

6.   You will be standing in line with (who, <u>whom</u>)?

7.   The big race was won by my team and (they, <u>them</u>).

8.   (<u>He</u>, Him) and my sister are returning to college soon.

9.   Each of the winners (<u>receives</u>, receive) a ribbon.

10.   Neither of the uniforms (<u>displays</u>, display) the right logo.

Quiz #10

1.   Frank and (<u>he</u>, him) went to the store for their mother.

2.   (Who, <u>Whom</u>) did you select for your team?

3.   We brought travel brochures for his sister and (he, <u>him</u>).

4.   Mom and (<u>I</u>, me) will be arriving at the party a little later.

5.   Everybody on the team will need to wear (<u>his</u>, their) uniform for the picture.

6.   From (who, <u>whom</u>) have they already received an answer?

7.   They all wanted to come with (we, <u>us</u>) band members.

8.   The new co-captains were Sharon and (<u>she</u>, her).

9.   A full meal was provided for the contestants and (they, <u>them</u>).

10.   Each of the girls (<u>has</u>, have) a different project for science.

Quiz #11

1.   Has everyone in the group brought (<u>his</u>, their) poster?

2.   (<u>Who</u>, whom) will lead the parade on Saturday?

3.   My best friend and (<u>she</u>, her) are coming over in an hour.

4.   The person at the door might be (<u>she</u>, her).

5.   Neither of the books (<u>fits</u>, fit) in the locker.

6.   By (who, <u>whom</u>) was that book written?

7.   My mother prepared a birthday feast for my father and (I, <u>me</u>).

8.   Each of the orders (<u>contains</u>, contain) three egg rolls.

9.   No one had prepared (<u>his</u>, their) outline properly.

10.   (Who, <u>Whom</u>) had the team chosen as captain?

Quiz #12

1. About (who, <u>whom</u>) was that story written?

2. My mother and (<u>he</u>, him) went to wait in line for tickets.

3. They presented the trophy to Mr. Smith and (we, <u>us</u>).

4. Nobody remembered to bring (<u>his</u>, their) bathing suit.

5. (<u>Who</u>, Whom) will present the award to the recipient?

6. Two of the team members were Sally and (<u>she</u>, her).

7. Each of the tires on the car (<u>was</u>, were) flat.

8. In the afternoon she and (<u>I</u>, me) will be going home.

9. (Who, <u>Whom</u>) will the cast select as the lead in the play?

10. To Sharon and (I, <u>me</u>), the room looked beautiful.

Quiz #13

1. No one could believe (<u>his</u>, their) eyes.

2. The two new committee members were my father and (<u>I</u>, me).

3. Neither of the girls (<u>plays</u>, play) on my team.

4. To (who, <u>whom</u>) did you address the letter?

5. Everyone easily remembered (<u>his</u>, their) position in line.

6. (<u>Who</u>, whom) will coach our new team?

7. The new co-captains will be Sharon and (<u>he</u>, him).

8. Each of the boxes (<u>looks</u>, look) exactly the same.

9. Jerry and (<u>he</u>, him) should thank the hosts of the party.

10. (Who, <u>Whom</u>) will the boss hire for the new position?

Quiz #14

1. My mother gave the gift to Frank and (she, <u>her</u>).

2. The counselors and (<u>they</u>, them) sponsored the event together.

3. Either of those two students (<u>runs</u>, run) faster than I do.

4. (<u>Who</u>, Whom) will lead our team to victory?

5. Everything belongs in (<u>its</u>, their) place.

6. From my friend and (they, <u>them</u>) I received three recommendations.

7. We brought uniforms for the team and (he, <u>him</u>).

8. My father and (<u>I</u>, me) arrived at the same time.

9. Near (who, <u>whom</u>) will you be standing?

10. Each of the girls (<u>reminds</u>, remind) me of her mother.

Quiz #15

1. She and (<u>he</u>, him) went to the new theater.

2. Each of the boys (<u>has</u>, have) a different job.

3. The grand prize winners were Sam and (<u>I</u>, me).

4. Nobody wanted to give up (<u>his</u>, their) seat.

5. The race was between Francis and (he, <u>him</u>).

6. Neither of the teams (<u>has</u>, have) a perfect record.

7.   She and (<u>we</u>, us) were the last to leave.

8.   Several of the new students (was, <u>were</u>) talking to the principal.

9.   To Lori and (she, <u>her</u>), the whole day was special.

10.   My mother and (<u>I</u>, me) went to the bank after school.

Quiz #16

1.   Each of the winners (<u>was</u>, were) announced over the loudspeaker.

2.   Ethan and (<u>I</u>, me) went out for an early dinner.

3.   From (who, <u>whom</u>) did you receive a check?

4.   The gardener showed my sister and (she, <u>her</u>) how to plant the seeds.

5.   The last speakers were the club president and (<u>he</u>, him).

6.   Everyone in the room was moving quickly toward (<u>his</u>, their) seat.

7.   (<u>Who</u>, Whom) is the next competitor?

8.   Neither of the students (<u>has</u>, have) enough money for the card.

9.   Sheila and (<u>they</u>, them) entered as a team.

10.   Either of the boys (<u>has</u>, have) the right to go with us.

Quiz #17

1.   (<u>Who</u>, Whom) will bring the refreshments for the party?

2.   They decided to come with my brother and (we, <u>us</u>).

3.   No one could decide to (who, <u>whom</u>) they should send the gift.

4.   (<u>Who</u>, Whom) was elected president of the club?

5.   Much of the grass (<u>has</u>, have) dried up.

6.   Everybody wanted to take (<u>his</u>, their) things to the room.

7.   Give that book to the teacher or (she, <u>her</u>).

8.   My brother and (<u>I</u>, me) ordered pizza for dinner.

9.   By (who, <u>whom</u>) will you sit at the assembly?

10.   All of the books (has, <u>have</u>) been returned.

Quiz #18

1.   Each of the three boys (<u>appears</u>, appear) nervous.

2.   Either of those buses (<u>stops</u>, stop) near your house.

3.   My family and (<u>she</u>, her) will be going on vacation together.

4.   Everyone remembered to bring (<u>his</u>, their) jacket to camp.

5.   About (who, <u>whom</u>) are you speaking?

6.   The prizes were given to Sue and (he, <u>him</u>).

7.   Neither of the dogs had worn (<u>its</u>, their) collar.

8.   They and (<u>we</u>, us) were the next groups in line.

9.   (Who, <u>Whom</u>) did you send to collect the materials?

10.   No one in the room could remember (<u>his</u>, their) goal.

Quiz #19

1. Neither of the men could accept (<u>his</u>, their) award.

2. Much of the delicious soup (<u>was</u>, were) already gone.

3. My brother and (<u>he</u>, him) are at camp for the summer.

4. Each of the members (<u>plans</u>, plan) to attend.

5. For Sarah and (I, <u>me</u>), this day will never end.

6. Everyone in the class needs (<u>his</u>, their) own books.

7. They appeared on stage with Amelia and (we, <u>us</u>).

8. Her mother and (<u>she</u>, her) will enter their drawings in the contest.

9. Either of the answers (<u>is</u>, are) correct.

10. Someone on the team lost (<u>her</u>, their) shoes.

Quiz #20

1. (Who, <u>Whom</u>) can the people trust?

2. Neither of my friends (<u>is</u>, are) going to the party.

3. We gave that job to Sean and (he, <u>him</u>).

4. The next person in line was (<u>she</u>, her).

5. To (who, <u>whom</u>) is that package being sent?

6. Each of those plants (<u>requires</u>, require) a great deal of sun.

7. My sister and (<u>she</u>, her) will return to college soon.

8. Either of the boys (<u>rides</u>, ride) very well.

9. Everyone in the class needs to show (<u>his</u>, their) ticket now.

10. Few of the papers (was, <u>were</u>) returned.

Section III: VERBS

Chapter 11: Recognizing Verbs

The following quizzes will review verbs. Included in this section will be verbs and verb phrases in sentences; recognizing transitive and intransitive verbs; recognizing action, state-of-being, and linking verbs; identifying verb tenses; and identifying active and passive voice.

In the first section, each quiz will consist of ten sentences containing verbs of *one* to *four* words. In a properly written sentence, there can be no more than three helping verbs and a main verb. Like the noun portion of this book, the number of words in each verb will be noted at the end of the sentence and can be given to aid in recognition of the verb if so desired. The words in the verb will appear in italics. Sentences in question form will often have a helping verb at the beginning.

Students will write the verbs from each sentence on their papers. Never include the "n't" in contractions or any other adverbs as part of the verb.

Quiz #1

1. *Should* my family *have stayed* one more night? (3)

2. They *will* never *arrive* on time. (2)

3. No one *should* ever *have been driving* that fast. (4)

4. *Did* the captain of the team really *win* a trophy? (2)

5. *Can't* we *go* with you? (2)

6. You *must* always *prepare* for a test. (2)

7. He *might* even *be* the overall winner. (2)

8. *Don't roam* too far from camp. (2)

9. He *has* usually *had* much better luck in that event. (2)

10. *Will* the train to the city *be leaving* soon? (3)

Quiz #2

1. *Can* my new friend from school *come* with us? (2)

2. She *may* soon *become* the leader of the whole group. (2)

3. They *might* not *have seen* him. (3)

4. *Should*n't the security patrol *have been checking* all the doors? (4)

5. My windows *were rattling* loudly in the strong wind. (2)

6. *Don't* the others in your group *want* a sandwich, too? (2)

7. You *must* really *like* your job. (2)

8. *Am* I always the first one here? (1)

9. The deer *was* silently *running* across the large meadow. (2)

10. *Would*n't my sister *have brought* it with her? (3)

Quiz #3

1. When *will* this job *be finished*? (3)

2. *Should* we *have arrived* a little later? (3)

3. He *may have been leaving* right after the concert. (4)

4. The others from my neighborhood *could* not *have left* yet. (3)

5. Many of us *have* not yet *begun* our project. (2)

6. You *must* never *leave* them alone. (2)

7. *Wouldn't* you *like* a piece of chocolate cake? (2)

8. They *must have gone* home early. (3)

9. He *did* not *do* his homework until after nine o'clock. (2)

10. They *would* not *have been returning* at such a late hour. (4)

Quiz #4

1. *Can* you *go* to the movie with us? (2)

2. The drama productions *will* almost always *start* on time. (2)

3. Those boys *could* not *have been going* to the game. (4)

4. *Did* the blue jays in the large oak tree ever *finish* their nest? (2)

5. Her sister *should* easily *be* home by 2 o'clock. (2)

6. *Must* you always *arrive* late? (2)

7. He *has* not *had* a very easy time this year. (2)

8. The band members *do* not *want* any ice cream. (2)

9. That group *might be performing* in the pavilion at noon. (3)

10. *Have* the students from the other class *selected* a team yet? (2)

Quiz #5

1. *May* the rest of the group *follow* us? (2)

2. You *could* always *come* back tomorrow. (2)

3. *Will* the children from the other school *be coming* with us? (3)

4. You *can* never again *change* your decision. (2)

5. *Could* that man at the head of the line *have* already *registered*? (3)

6. *Must* we always *have* tests on Friday? (2)

7. *Should* the other group *have been performing* on Tuesday?

8. All the noise *stopped* at midnight. (1)

9. We *would* really *like* a different schedule this week. (2)

10. The new game *might* actually *begin* on time. (2)

Quiz #6

1. *May* I *go* with them to her performance? (2)

2. *Should*n't he *have been watching* more closely? (4)

3. We *could* not *have done* it without you. (3)

4. *Will* the players on my team *be receiving* any recognition? (3)

5. All of the students *must have arrived* on time. (3)

6. They *will* already *have left* by three. (3)

7. We *have* not *had* any rain recently. (2)

8. She *can* always *wait* for you out in front of the school. (2)

9. He *might be bringing* it to us later. (3)

10. That *would* really *have caused* too much trouble. (3)

Quiz #7

1. Someone *was searching* for the pearl. (2)

2. They *might have been waiting* for the authorities. (4)

3. The sun *rose* quickly in the sky. (1)

4. Five boys *will be chosen* for the trip. (3)

5. The new cars *are arriving* at the dealership. (2)

6. *Stop* near the bench on the corner. (1)

7. *Did* the children *listen* carefully to the story? (2)

8. The boat *will be sailing* from the dock at noon. (3)

9. Musicians *should* always *practice* before a performance. (2)

10. No one *could have finished* the job any earlier. (3)

Quiz #8

1. They *should* really *have tried* much harder. (3)

2. *Would* the rest of the work *have been finished* by Monday? (4)

3. He *could* not *complete* the big project on time. (2)

4. *Must* he always *be* the best? (2)

5. The new lines *were being sprayed* on the field. (3)

6. *Don't* the members of the choir *have* a practice today? (2)

7. They *will* immediately *be returning* to California. (3)

8. *Should* your neighbor from across the street *have been watering* the grass every day? (4)

9. *Could* the rest of the team *stay* for the presentations? (2)

10. They *might* soon *change* their minds. (2)

Quiz #9

1. *May* we please *come* with you? (2)

2. He *will* not ever *remember* that assignment. (2)

3. *Should*n't the other members of the team *have been practicing* also? (4)

4. They *could* always *be sold* at a later auction. (3)

5. The new posters *would* not *stick* to the shiny surface. (2)

6. *Has* the new proposal for the stadium already *been discussed* with the owners? (3)

7. The boys *might* really *have been delayed* by the weather. (4)

8. From their window they *must* easily *have seen* the whole event. (3)

9. He *could* not possibly *have left* home yet. (3)

10. She *will promise* me anything. (2)

Quiz #10

1. *Should* that bell *have rung* so early? (3)

2. They *might have entered* the contest on their own. (3)

3. *Did* the students in the band *wear* a different uniform? (2)

4. They *could* easily *have returned* it by today. (3)

5. The children *should* not *have been playing* outside today. (4)

6. *Will* the next train to the city *be coming* soon? (3)

7. He *can* always *be located* in the business directory. (3)

8. *May* your three children *come* with us tomorrow? (2)

9. The larger box *must have been thrown* away. (4)

10. Don't the prices almost always *dip* after Christmas? (2)

Quiz #11

1. *Did* all of the boys in our class *make* the team? (2)

2. *Could* the plane *have arrived* an hour early? (3)

3. You *might* never *have been chosen* at all. (4)

4. These events *will* always *begin* on time. (2)

5. The children *have* not *been playing* with their new toys. (3)

6. *Doesn't* the program in the gym *continue* for another hour? (2)

7. All the performers *should* already *have been changing* for the next scene. (4)

8. *Would*n't the old clothes from the box in the attic *make* great costumes? (2)

9. The students *must* not always *borrow* the school's equipment. (2)

10. None of the cars *should* ever *have run* out of gas. (3)

Quiz #12

1. *Shall* we *go* to the performance tonight? (2)

2. You *should*n't *arrive* after eight o'clock. (2)

3. When *will* all of his friends *be leaving* for the play? (3)

4. You *could have been planning* the trip to the capital months ago. (4)

5. They *will* always *remember* their first visit. (2)

6. The trip up the mountain *must* actually *begin* at the head of that trail. (2)

7. *May* we now *complete* our original plan? (2)

8. The group *stopped* near the door of the library. (1)

9. A few of the boys *might have won* the grand prize. (3)

10. *Can* we possibly *find* another team member? (2)

Quiz #13

1. *Will* they all *go* to the play together? (2)

2. *Don't* the members of the club *need* transportation? (2)

3. Those girls *might* never *have* this opportunity again. (2)

4. *Must* the counselors and staff also *take* sleeping bags? (2)

5. What *could* the team *have done* differently? (3)

6. He *should* not *have been following* so closely. (4)

7. You *must* always *ask* your parents first. (2)

8. *Would* everyone in the group *like* a cold soda? (2)

9. *Did*n't my letter *arrive* before the deadline? (2)

10. They *may* not actually *want* all of the equipment. (2)

Quiz #14

1. *Has* everyone in the group *brought* his project? (2)

2. I *shall* soon *become* a member of that new club. (2)

3. *Did*n't they *choose* a different color for the decorations? (2)

4. They *would* never *have been called* in time for the meeting. (4)

5. *Were* the members of the basketball team *practicing* this morning? (2)

6. He *should* really *have been included* in that new group. (4)

7. *May* my best friends and I *join* you for the movie? (2)

8. My sister *could* always *have found* a good restaurant here. (3)

9. *Will* all of the girls on the committee *need* a sponsor? (2)

10. It *might* only *need* a bit more paint. (2)

Quiz #15

1. *Did* he *run* in the race on Saturday? (2)

2. He *must have gone* to the store on the corner earlier. (3)

3. *Will* the coach of our team *cancel* the game? (2)

4. You *should* never *have called* her so late. (3)

5. *Could* my brother's team *have been playing* at the same time? (4)

6. *May* my little sister *come* with us to the mall? (2)

7. Her mother *would* not *have left* her alone in the house. (3)

8. *Do* the students in our class *have* a math test tomorrow? (2)

9. You *can* always *ride* to the game with us. (2)

10. The wind *was blowing* steadily from the north. (2)

Quiz #16

1. *Could* you *stop* by my house this afternoon? (2)

2. He *would* never *have been studying* there that late. (4)

3. *May* the students in our group *go* last? (2)

4. The group from our school *must have taken* an earlier train. (3)

5. The crew *will* not ever *finish* their project on time. (2)

6. *Do* all of the tables in the room *have* place cards? (2)

7. My mother *is* always *driving* our team to games after school. (2)

8. We *should* not *have been standing* so close to the track. (4)

9. *Did* he *remember* his homework? (2)

10. She *will have had* four tests by the end of the day. (3)

Quiz #17

1. *Shall* I *begin* the program now? (2)

2. You *should* never *have left* them behind. (3)

3. *Aren't* the others in your group *making* cupcakes for snacks? (2)

4. *May* all of us on the team *arrive* early for practice? (2)

5. The city roads *could* not *handle* two feet of snow. (2)

6. The coach *was* quickly *preparing* the team roster for the announcer. (2)

7. They *will* not *have run* the entire course by that time. (2)

8. You *can* almost always *find* a great gift at that store. (2)

9. We *should* not *have been starting* again at such a late date. (4)

10. The team members *had* not *had* enough sleep between games. (2)

Quiz #18

1. *Will* the game *be running* late tonight? (3)

2. *Have* the new sofa and chairs for the dining room *been delivered*? (3)

3. Nothing *would* ever *have changed* his mind about the project. (3)

4. *Do* all of your books from school *fit* in your locker? (2)

5. She *has* always *had* a very positive attitude. (2)

6. They *might* not *be leaving* until later this afternoon. (3)

7. *Shouldn't* we *have been stopped* before that last gate? (4)

8. We *shall* never ever *forget* our last trip to Europe. (2)

9. She *is* not *amending* her plans for the birthday party. (2)

10. We *may* actually *go* there again this afternoon. (2)

Quiz #19

1. *Has* the pouring rain *leaked* through the front window? (2)

2. They *might* already *have entered* by another door. (3)

3. *Was*n't he *finished* with the meeting before lunch? (2)

4. We *can* always *return* the books to the library tomorrow. (2)

5. *Shall* I *continue* with the list now? (2)

6. The team *should* not *have been arriving* so late. (4)

7. The wind *howled* noisily through the vacant house. (1)

8. Your friend *might* not *want* a part in the play. (2)

9. *Could* they ever *have imagined* such a crowd? (3)

10. By the ticket booth, a long line *was* already *forming.* (2)

Quiz #20

1. *Will* the rain *have stopped* by game time? (3)

2. *May* the members of my committee *use* the same forms? (2)

3. They *would* not ever *have tried* that by themselves. (3)

4. He *should* really not *be doing* that right now. (3)

5. My friends *have been* carefully *searching* for hours. (3)

6. He *has created* that problem for himself. (2)

7. *Might* the group from the other side of town *arrive* slightly later? (2)

8. *Has* the water in the fountain at the mall *been replaced* yet? (3)

9. We *shall* never *make* it to the show on time. (2)

10. He *can* always *remember* the names of everyone on the list. (2)

Quiz #21

1. *Shouldn't* all the members of the team *be riding* the same bus? (3)

2. Nothing *could* ever *disturb* him during his lectures. (2)

3. The children *would* never *have left* without us. (3)

4. *Must* the older students *ride* with the younger students? (2)

5. *Will* all of the plans for the theater *be* ready by Friday? (2)

6. The group *may have been saving* their best performance for the end. (4)

7. He *might* not *be calling* until tomorrow evening. (3)

8. That schedule *does* not usually *work* for this group of parents. (2)

9. We *should have* already *planned* the activities for that event. (3)

10. *Guide* the students through the maze. (1)

Quiz #22

1. *Should*n't he *be running* on the team with us? (3)

2. At three o'clock they *must have left* the game. (3)

3. *Was*n't the man with your father *checking* our new product? (2)

4. She *might* not *have called* us at all. (3)

5. The group *was* always *listed* in the top five. (2)

6. *Could* the members of our small group *join* your group? (2)

7. The speeding car *could* not easily *stop* at the red light. (2)

8. The small gym *will* hardly *hold* the team and their fans. (2)

9. A large number of students *will* usually *be competing* in games after school. (3)

10. The rain showers *had* finally *passed* out of the area. (2)

Quiz #23

1. *May* the captains of both teams *be dismissed* five minutes early? (3)

2. They *will* never *finish* that project in two hours. (2)

3. *Have* all of the players *had* a chance at the free weights? (2)

4. Some of us *might* not ever *get* another opportunity like this one. (2)

5. *Bring* all of your equipment with you to the track. (1)

6. The whole group *should* never *have been standing* that close. (4)

7. *Was* the sun *shining* earlier this morning? (2)

8. *Does* each member of the committee *want* the same thing? (2)

9. They *could have arrived* sooner except for the heavy traffic. (3)

10. You *can* almost always *depend* upon our team captain. (2)

Quiz #24

1. *Could* we please *see* the scores of all the teams? (2)

2. They *should have been staying* with their grandparents. (4)

3. *Didn't* he *bring* his books with him to the library? (2)

4. My friends in the dorm *will* always *leave* the lights on for us. (2)

5. My sister *might be coming* home from college tomorrow. (3)

6. *Was* that flock of geese *flying* in formation? (2)

7. *Can't* the members of the refreshment committee *bring* sodas? (2)

8. The train to downtown *does* not always *run* on time. (2)

9. The small bird in the palm tree *was* quietly *singing*. (2)

10. He *must have been trying* very hard on his homework. (4)

Quiz #25

1. *Could* the students from the other school *have joined* our group? (3)

2. *May* we *go* with you to the movie? (2)

3. They *must* not *have seen* any of the game after halftime. (3)

4. She *should have been preparing* for that test all week. (4)

5. *Did*n't the boy in the green jersey *win* both races? (2)

6. He *slowed* the car in front of the market. (1)

7. She *may return* from her trip as early as tomorrow. (2)

8. *Is* the newest member of the club *bringing* brownies? (2)

9. The girls *have* always *been* on time to these meetings. (2)

10. We *could* not possibly *have known* the final results by the end of the day. (3)

Quiz #26

1. *Should* the boys *be waiting* in line for over an hour? (3)

2. *Don't* we *want* lunches for the trip, too? (2)

3. They *must have discovered* the problem with the electricity too late. (3)

4. *Will* the children in the park on the slide *be included*, also? (3)

5. The decision *might* not *be* that easy. (2)

6. The leaves on the trees *may* soon *be turning* autumn colors. (3)

7. No one *would* ever *have been waiting* that long. (4)

8. My best friend *is* always *studying* for something. (2)

9. *Might* we *tag* along with you to the mall? (2)

10. That car *has stopped* in front of my house. (2)

Quiz #27

1. *Join* us for dinner later. (1)

2. *Don't* you *want* the final assignment for the project? (2)

3. The people from the store *should have called* us by now. (3)

4. They *must* always *begin* at the corner by the stadium. (2)

5. Our two dogs *are* never *left* in the car in the heat. (2)

6. The restaurant manager *might have been showing* you another way. (4)

7. *Shouldn't* the girls in that group *be* ahead of us? (2)

8. You *can* always *call* your mother from the game. (2)

9. The candles *had been burning* brightly on the side table. (3)

10. She *has been wearing* a different shade of pink each day. (3)

Quiz #28

1. *Could*n't you *come* with us to the game tonight? (2)

2. The driver *might* not ever *be stopping* the bus there again. (3)

3. You *must have been going* the other direction. (4)

4. *Were*n't you *correcting* your tests? (2)

5. No one *should* ever *have made* so many mistakes. (3)

6. My friends from school *will be arriving* early in the morning. (3)

7. *Have* they *been following* that team's record? (3)

8. *Show* me the article in the magazine. (1)

9. *Must* the trip to the mall *take* so long? (2)

10. *Do* you always *bring* those tools with you? (2)

Quiz #29

1. *Did* anyone from our class *run* in the marathon? (2)

2. The seniors in the class *will* always *challenge* the juniors. (2)

3. Someone *could* easily *have been hiding* in that closet. (4)

4. When *do* the other three *come* home? (2)

5. The students *must remember* their money for the pictures. (2)

6. *May* we *have* a ride to the game tonight? (2)

7. Where *shall* I *sit* for the performance? (2)

8. The car *should* not *be started* for at least an hour. (3)

9. Anyone *might have saved* that pile of papers. (3)

10. The small child *cried* for most of the night. (1)

Quiz #30

1. She *shouldn't be running* with those scissors. (3)

2. No one *could hear* a sound from the vacant house. (2)

3. Why *don't* you *stay* for the basketball game after school? (2)

4. My family *may be going* to California tomorrow. (3)

5. *Will* you *be coming* with us to the movies tonight? (3)

6. They *did* not *stop* at the store on the way home. (2)

7. You *should have been trying* harder on your tests. (4)

8. Can't the boys and girls in her class *begin* sooner? (2)

9. They *sang* the songs together. (1)

10. The exhibit *will* very soon *be opening* in our hometown. (3)

Chapter 12: Transitive and Intransitive

In the following quizzes, students will be determining whether the verb in each sentence is *transitive* or *intransitive*. A transitive verb will always take a direct object (answers *whom* or *what* to the verb), and an intransitive verb will be a linking verb followed by a predicate noun or adjective or an action verb alone or followed by phrases or adverbs, but no complement. If there is nothing but a phrase, adverb, or period following the verb, it is intransitive. **If the sentence has a direct object, it is transitive; if it does not, it is intransitive**. Some verbs, such as *arrive,* are always intransitive.

Both the verb and whether it is transitive or intransitive will be shown in each sentence in this section. Students can simply write "T" or "I" or include the verb as well.

Quiz #1

1. The three swans *floated* peacefully on the lake's surface. (I)

2. My mother *was* the chairman of the committee. (I)

3. The captains *chose* their last players. (T)

4. The three students *recited* their poems for the class. (T)

5. We *drove* to the mall on Saturday. (I)

6. On our vacation we *went* to Disneyland. (I)

7. The runners *were* extremely tired after the race. (I)

8. The eager girl *set* her alarm for 7 A.M. (T)

9. The chairs *were* in a stack by the back door. (I)

10. The students *trudged* slowly to school through the snow. (I)

Quiz #2

1. *What average *do* you *have* in history? (T)

2. He *was walking* on the sidewalk near school. (I)

3. Our plane *will arrive* home early this evening. (I)

4. She *should have been* the winner of that event. (I)

5. My mother *has picked* flowers for the centerpiece on the table. (T)

6. They *strolled* leisurely around the museum. (I)

7. By the end of the test, her mind *was* completely *drained*. (I)

8. The fierce winds *howled* loudly through the tall pines. (I)

9. Each person *practiced* for the performance for three hours. (I)

10. From the outside the house *appeared* dark and empty. (I)

Quiz #3

1. He quickly *shoved* his books into the locker. (T)

2. My sister *has taken* the dog for a walk around the neighborhood. (T)

3. She *will be* the winner of every race. (I)

4. The committee members *walked* angrily toward the door. (I)

5. The girls quickly *swam* across the pool. (I)

6. The bus *has pulled* into the parking lot of the school. (I)

7. *There *were* numerous rose bushes in the garden. (I)

8. The beautiful kite *flew* high in the air. (I)

9. The summer temperatures *have been* very warm. (I)

10. *Did* all the students *enter* the contest? (T)

Quiz #4

1. In the middle of the field, a small rabbit *popped* up from its burrow. (I)

2. A large flock of geese *flew* over the meadow. (I)

3. My father *will be purchasing* a new car on Saturday. (T)

4. That new student *is* a teammate of mine. (I)

5. Nobody *has bought* drinks for the party. (T)

6. He *was pushing* the loaded cart down every aisle. (T)

7. Their plane *should arrive* at the terminal on time. (I)

8. A light breeze *blew* across the surface of the lake. (I)

9. The small boy *became* extremely frightened in the dark. (I)

10. The amateur group *will perform* first tonight. (I)

Quiz #5

1. He *has borrowed* a book from his friend. (T)

2. My mother *will be* back in the morning. (I)

3. *Will* they *be returning* before the second half? (I)

4. A young woman *was pushing* a baby stroller along the street. (T)

5. The team *became* very excited at the good news. (I)

6. The four students *arrived* home before their parents. (I)

7. The small dog *ran* around and around the yard. (I)

8. That girl *was* my best friend in elementary school. (I)

9. My father *is buying* my sister a new car this weekend. (T)

10. *Did* the heavy rain *ruin* the crops on your uncle's farm? (T)

Quiz #6

1. The first bell of the school year *rang* at 8:30. (I)

2. The students in every class *were assigned* a song in Spanish. (T)

3. No one *could see* the ship in the thick fog. (T)

4. *Bring* a pencil and your calculator for your math test. (T)

5. *Stop* at the crosswalk. (I)

6. The captain of the team *spoke* in a very loud voice. (I)

7. We *rode* to the nearest mall for some ice cream. (I)

8. He *has erased* the answers from the board. (T)

9. No one *could spell* the word correctly. (T)

10. All of the students *ran* around the block three times. (I)

Quiz #7

1. He *could* not *carry* the heavy box by himself. (T)

2. *Has* your brother *become* the new football coach? (I)

3. *Can* someone *help* me with the last fence post? (T)

4. A large flock of geese *flew* across the cloudless sky. (I)

5. *Did* anyone in our group *write* the last poem? (T)

6. The spring weather *had turned* very cold. (I)

7. Over the tops of the trees *sailed* a large bouquet of balloons. (I)

8. She *could* always *bring* them to my house. (T)

9. A narrow path *wound* through the dark woods. (I)

10. *Were* the flags *blowing* in the steady wind? (I)

Quiz #8

1. The small brown dog *ran* quickly over the hill. (I)

2. The boy *should have caught* the ball at the fence. (T)

3. We *shall eat* oranges and bananas for a snack. (T)

4. The young man *carried* our suitcases to the plane. (T)

5. Black clouds *appeared* in the sky. (I)

6. No one *was interested* in any of the first results. (I)

7. They *threw* the smaller rocks onto the pile. (T)

8. My mother *is cooking* eggs and bacon for breakfast. (T)

9. The large trees in my yard *swayed* in the steady breeze. (I)

10. The small group of skydivers *jumped* nervously from the plane. (I)

Quiz #9

1. They *should have arrived* at the airport sooner. (I)

2. By the end of the week, he *will have planted* twenty trees. (T)

3. *Don't* you *love* chocolate chip ice cream? (T)

4. The bald eagle *is rising* on that current of wind. (I)

5. We *could have left* our coats in the car. (T)

6. No one *was* tired after the dance competition. (I)

7. They *can fly* through the air with the greatest of ease. (I)

8. During the night the rain *was pounding* loudly on the roof. (I)

9. It *will* hardly *fit* in the small box. (I)

10. The children *have been running* in circles around the yard. (I)

Quiz #10

1. The three girls *entered* the new race this morning. (T)

2. She *could* not *hide* the joy in her face. (T)

3. White, billowy clouds *were racing* across the sky. (I)

4. My brother *will* soon *be calling* with the good news. (I)

5. Nothing *could have stopped* the rushing flood waters. (T)

6. The fly ball *should have landed* out of bounds. (I)

7. The class *selected* three different stories for discussion. (T)

8. The president *must have been pounding* the gavel on the podium. (T)

9. The tables *were* easily *moved* to one side. (I)

10. The eager student *is studying* for a science test. (I)

Quiz #11

1. He *was walking* over the hill to the meadow. (I)

2. Beautiful wildflowers *will be growing* on every hillside. (I)

3. He *must have made* a call to his father from the pay phone. (T)

4. Both planes *might be arriving* at the same time. (I)

5. We *have* already *brought* cookies and doughnuts. (T)

6. They *could* never *have ridden* to the end of the course. (I)

7. *Didn't* the students in the class *choose* a different cover? (T)

8. They *might* always *return* at that time of the year. (I)

9. Each day they *run* through the park and across the bridge. (I)

10. The students *will have returned* all books by Friday. (T)

Quiz #12

1. *Must* the telephone always *ring* so early in the morning? (I)

2. We really *should have brought* warmer clothes. (T)

3. He *walked* anxiously into the crowded auditorium. (I)

4. They *may* not even *arrive* until this afternoon. (I)

5. *Did*n't the club's officers *hold* a successful bake sale? (T)

6. The wind *has been blowing* dust around the valley all night. (T)

7. The boys *could*n't *have worked* any harder. (I)

8. He *could* easily *be heard* at the edge of the crowd. (I)

9. The team *will* probably *be playing* for another hour. (I)

10. We *can* always *return* to the event later. (I)

Quiz #13

1. She *should have been* the final contestant. (I)

2. *May* the members of the team *leave* at three o'clock? (I)

3. He *could* never *have run* ten miles. (T)

4. *Will* the bell for the dismissal of class *be ringing* soon? (I)

5. The group *has* very carefully *chosen* a new president. (T)

6. My friend *might have been playing* at the other field. (I)

7.   She *will* always *be* a very special person. (I)

8.   That team *can* almost always *play* at a moment's notice. (I)

9.   *Could*n't they *have called* before ten o'clock? (I)

10.   The trees in our yard *were* wildly *blowing* in the strong wind (I)

Quiz #14

1.   The police *chased* the robber through the streets. (T)

2.   She *could have entered* the high school competition. (T)

3.   *Don't* you *swim* in the mornings? (I)

4.   Every morning he *will walk* his dog in the park. (T)

5.   We *should have arrived* at the mall by three. (I)

6.   She *can* always *leave* early in the morning. (I)

7.   The ships in the harbor *were* lost in the fog. (I)

8.   They *might have grabbed* the wrong book. (T)

9.   For dessert my mother *must be making* cookies. (T)

10.   The group *will be singing* there for three days. (I)

Quiz #15

1.   They *walked* all night through the forest. (I)

2.   Both boys on the team *were* leaders. (I)

3.   He *should have kicked* the ball away from the goal. (T)

4.   That *would* not *have prevented* the accident. (T)

5.   The lion *must have roared* very loudly. (I)

6.   The vase on the table *did*n't *fall* during the struggle. (I)

7.   The final game *is* tomorrow at noon. (I)

8.   Six monkeys *should enter* the cage at any moment. (T)

9.   *Can't* they *give* you the money now? (T)

10.   The students *might be arriving* early for the track meet. (I)

Quiz #16

1.   The three boys *had* already *been* captains. (I)

2.   They *flew* down the hill on their bicycles. (I)

3.   They *did* not *deliver* the lunches until one o'clock. (T)

4.   A flock of Canadian geese *had landed* on the steep hillside. (I)

5.   The girls *will catch* the bus at the corner. (T)

6.   Nothing *could stop* the rushing river. (T)

7.   The small children in the yard *can* never *see* over the tall fence. (I)

8.   He *should* not *drive* quickly through the crowded streets. (I)

9.   My mother *has carried* the groceries from the car. (T)

10.   Our group *should be performing* there by next week. (I)

Quiz #17

1.   My mother *will call* tomorrow. (I)

2.	After the tryouts the students *were* extremely tired. (I)

3.	All morning she *had been swimming* in their new pool. (I)

4.	No one *can understand* the words to that song. (T)

5.	He quickly *pushed* his dirty clothes under the bed. (T)

6.	We *should have shopped* for it yesterday. (I)

7.	They *will* probably *be* the stars of the show. (I)

8.	The judges *could have announced* the winners sooner. (T)

9.	Most students *do* not *enjoy* tests in any subject. (T)

10.	Do*n't* those people *care* about the new show? (I)

Quiz #18

1.	They all *ran* quickly out the front door. (I)

2.	By the stream *were* three boys on a large rock. (I)

3.	A loud crash *could be heard* from the hallway. (I)

4.	With their mother's help, the boys *packed* a large picnic lunch. (T)

5.	The student *had asked* a very important question. (T)

6.	My best friend *was* the next performer on the stage. (I)

7.	Nothing *could interfere* with their plans for the afternoon. (I)

8.	The coach *shouted* loudly to all the members of his team. (I)

9. His father *brought* the new car around to the front of the house. (T)

10. The wind *blew* fiercely through the tall pines. (I)

Quiz #19

1. The sun *rose* brilliantly over the hills. (I)

2. You *should have brought* different shoes with you. (T)

3. The student *carried* his books in his backpack. (T)

4. The paper airplane *disappeared* in a ditch at the end of the field. (I)

5. Beautiful flowers *were growing* by the back wall. (I)

6. He *hung* his wet jacket on a hook behind the door. (T)

7. The excited young girl *rode* her new bicycle to the mall. (T)

8. The spring sky *was filled* with fluffy clouds. (I)

9. A huge puddle *lay* across the entire sidewalk. (I)

10. He *has chosen* hamburgers instead of hot dogs. (T)

Quiz #20

1. My mother *bought* groceries at the corner market. (T)

2. Many children *were playing* in the park by my house. (I)

3. Slowly, the group of young girls *walked* toward me. (I)

4. Debris *cluttered* the street after the storm. (T)

5. *Will* your sister *bring* your books to school? (T)

6. My friend *will be* the undisputed star of that team. (I)

7. Over the fields *raced* a large calico cat. (I)

8. The group *will perform* in three hours. (I)

9. The hikers easily *followed* the trail through the woods. (T)

10. Her parents *were* very tired after their trip. (I)

Quiz #21

1. *Will* he *ride* the bus tomorrow morning? (T)

2. The group *walked* very slowly from the room. (I)

3. A bright light *shone* through the window of the upstairs room. (I)

4. The tiny bird *hopped* away from the playful puppy. (I)

5. Soon, she *will be* the best player on the team. (I)

6. *May* we *take* pictures of the participants? (T)

7. She *practiced* for two hours on Saturday. (I)

8. A light breeze *rustled* softly through the trees. (I)

9. My mother *baked* brownies and pies for the carnival. (T)

10. The busboys *will carry* the dirty dishes to the kitchen. (T)

Quiz #22

1. The boys *have run* into the house for lunch. (I)

2. Everyone *was carrying* a duffel bag and a camera. (T)

3. She *shouted* loudly to her friends across the gym. (I)

4. Harriet Tubman *was* a conductor on the Underground Railroad. (I)

5. My parents *drove* around the city for two hours. (I)

6. Her brother *bought* a new bicycle on Saturday. (T)

7. They *hurried* toward their friends on the field. (I)

8. He *has become* the star of that movie. (I)

9. The frightened kitten *jumped* over the wall into the yard. (I)

10. We *chose* a new site for the party. (T)

Quiz #23

1. They *closed* the large window in the attic. (T)

2. The boys *walked* over the bridge and into the park. (I)

3. That lady *is* my mother's best friend. (I)

4. My friends and I *swam* across the small pond very quickly. (I)

5. My sister *was picking* flowers from the garden. (T)

6. She *loved* the birthday gifts from her family. (T)

7. The girls *were riding* their bicycles around the track. (T)

8. Her brother *has* already *become* a talented performer. (I)

9. His father *arrived* at the airport very late. (I)

10. The group *moved* quickly toward the bus. (I)

Quiz #24

1. *Has* he *brought* the books from the hallway? (T)

2. The girl in that picture *is* my next-door neighbor. (I)

3. They *walked* eagerly into the conference room. (I)

4. The track team *was running* toward the gym. (I)

5. *Will* she *bring* cookies for our dance? (T)

6. He easily *carried* his younger sister up the stairs. (T)

7. She *could* not *be* his partner for the project. (I)

8. The whole group *wandered* aimlessly about the room. (I)

9. The beautiful box kite *rose* high in the sky. (I)

10. They *will elect* a new president this week. (T)

Quiz #25

1. *Has* he *started* his homework yet? (T)

2. When *will* the others in the group *arrive*? (I)

3. The principal *will be ringing* the bell at nine o'clock. (T)

4. The two children *hid* behind a large tree in the yard. (I)

5. She *was* not a member of that committee. (I)

6. The dark clouds *moved* across the sky. (I)

7. The young man *glided* around the court easily. (I)

8. He *glanced* across the table at his friend. (I)

9. We *watched* a new program on TV last night. (T)

10. He *has bought* several tickets for his classmates. (T)

Quiz #26

1. They *watched* the final game on television. (T)

2. One day she *should be* a famous actress. (I)

3. *Will* the whole class *be* in our play? (I)

4. The soldiers *have captured* the enemy near the river. (T)

5. You *could have ridden* over to the mall. (I)

6. My brother *will be arriving* after the intermission. (I)

7. *Did* the team really *miss* the bus to the stadium? (T)

8. Her clothes *looked* elegant and practical. (I)

9. The students *had run* from the track to the gym. (I)

10. *Can* my new friend from school *stay* for dinner? (I)

Quiz #27

1. The large gray fox *escaped* quickly into the forest. (I)

2. She carefully *placed* the delicate vase on the counter. (T)

3. Her mother *bought* the ingredients for the cookies this morning. (T)

4. He *was* the best choice for the office. (I)

5. Our travel group *arrived* early at the airport for our trip. (I)

6. The high winds *blew* her hat from her head. (T)

7. Suddenly, a loud cry *broke* through the silence. (I)

8. The young athlete *won* third place in the state tournament. (T)

9. The crowd *moved* quickly toward the outer gate. (I)

10. He *has* always *been* worried about the project. (I)

Quiz #28

1. Dark smoke *rolled* quickly across the blue sky. (I)

2. The three ladies *walked* over the bridge to the city park. (I)

3. The rest of my family *arrived* in New York on Saturday. (I)

4. The speaker *approached* the podium with confidence. (T)

5. The squirrels *were nibbling* at the acorns beneath the tree. (I)

6. The coach of our team *is* my father. (I)

7. The workmen *opened* the attic door very cautiously. (T)

8. My brother *works* at the grocery store on the corner. (I)

9. That speech *was written* by a classmate of mine. (I)

10. He quite easily *reached* his destination before dark. (T)

Quiz #29

1. The children slowly *walked* toward the waiting bus. (I)

2. Her mother *was picking* flowers for the centerpiece. (T)

3. The entire audience *directed* its attention to the stage. (T)

4. A majestic eagle *soared* high above their heads. (I)

5. He *became* my closest friend and an excellent teammate. (I)

6. They desperately *searched* for the missing keys. (I)

7. We *must stop* at the store for bread and milk. (I)

8. He *called* his friends with the good news. (T)

9. We *crossed* over the river on the reopened bridge (I)

10. Our school band *marched* at the front of the parade. (I)

Quiz #30

1. They *walked* around the empty house quietly. (I)

2. *Did* she *ask* too many questions? (T)

3. My friend will never *return* her library books on time. (T)

4. Our team *is* the league champion. (I)

5. My little brother *climbed* up the tree to the roof. (I)

6. You *should show* them the plans for your project. (T)

7. I *shall arrive* early for some extra help. (I)

8. Dry leaves *blew* across the deserted playground. (I)

9. Her parents *called* after school on Friday. (I)

10. Her older sister *loves* the new color of her room. (T)

Quiz #31

1. The plane *circled* the airport for an hour. (T)

2. That artist *has painted* several pictures for the auction. (T)

3. My friend *waited* patiently by the auditorium door. (I)

4. She *has become* more talented with time. (I)

5. They *wrote* to the company for information. (I)

6. *Can* we *have* friends over for dinner? (T)

7. He *will be* a classmate of yours next year. (I)

8. The man *drove* carefully down the narrow street. (I)

9. The children *watched* a flock of geese on the water. (T)

10. They *were waiting* for a break in the traffic. (I)

Quiz #32

1. The small dog *ran* frantically around the table. (I)

2. She *was* the supervisor of our project. (T)

3. My brother *dragged* the lumber into the back yard. (T)

4. They *should have arrived* at that location on time. (I)

5. Her mother *is* responsible for desserts for the party. (I)

6. That student *gave* a great report on Helen Keller. (T)

7. We *were* amazed by the final score. (I)

8. She *will* always *be* the captain of our team. (I)

9. They *searched* the forest for honey and berries. (T)

10. On Sundays she *sings* in the church choir. (I)

Quiz #33

1. He *called* his mother from school. (T)

2. My new friend *is* very excited about her trip to New Mexico. (I)

3. My brother and his friends *will arrive* from college on Monday. (I)

4. The basketball team *practices* every day after school. (I)

5. The tiny kitten *rolled* the ball of yarn across the floor. (T)

6. A beautiful picture of his daughter *sat* on his desk. (I)

7. Her sister *has become* an associate in that firm. (I)

8. My friends *lay* in the sun for three hours. (I)

9. He *felt* very lucky in the competition. (I)

10. The smaller animals *hid* in the deep underbrush. (I)

Quiz #34

1. She *has become* the best player on the team. (I)

2. He *wandered* without purpose around the very large field. (I)

3. Our history class *is collecting* cans for recycling. (T)

4. He *arrived* at the game before the others. (I)

5. The tail of his long coat *was stuck* in the door. (I)

6. My older brother *is looking* for a job this summer. (I)

7. The doctor *examined* the boy's injuries carefully. (T)

8. The large dog *jumped* the fence with ease. (T)

9. She *will* always *be* honest. (I)

10. In science we *were testing* the theory of gravity. (T)

Chapter 13: Action, Linking, State-of-Being

In the following quizzes, students will be determining whether the verb in each sentence is an *action* verb, a *linking* verb, or a *state-of-being* verb. A verb can be an action verb whether the action is physical or mental. As long as some process is going on, the verb is showing action. A linking verb is intransitive and "links" the subject with either a noun, pronoun, or adjective in the predicate. The most common linking verb is *to be*, but other verbs, such as *become*, *seem*, *appear*, *taste*, *grow*, *feel*, and *smell* can also be linking verbs, depending upon their use. A state- of-being verb is always some form of the verb *to be*, but unlike a linking verb, it does not link to anything in the predicate. A state-of-being verb is usually followed by an adverb or a phrase but never by a predicate noun or predicate adjective.

Both the verb and its type will be shown in each sentence in this section. Students can write "A," "S," or "L." For extra practice they can also be asked to write the verb.

Quiz #1

1. They *could have danced* all night. (A)

2. The theater *was* very crowded for the early performance. (L)

3. My friend's father *is* a history teacher at his school. (L)

4. The famous painting *was* in a local gallery. (S)

5. We *rode* our bikes to the movies. (A)

6. You *were* here before us. (S)

7. The class *read* the story aloud. (A)

8. The whole room *became* dark and silent. (L)

9. They *stared* at the scene out the window. (A)

10. The chairs *were* in a row against the wall. (S)

Quiz #2

1. They *were running* into the house. (A)

2. On Saturday my mother *will become* president of that club. (L)

3. My best friend *is* in all of my classes at school. (S)

4. A row of large trees *was* in front of her house. (S)

5. He *was waiting* patiently for his mother. (A)

6. My father *is* the new assistant coach of that team. (L)

7. The rain *was falling* hard upon the ground. (A)

8. My sister *will be* in the play on Friday night. (S)

9. The whole group *disappeared* around the corner. (A)

10. She *seems* very unhappy with the results. (L)

Quiz #3

1. He *shouted* across the field to his friends. (A)

2. My father *is* in the office by the front door. (S)

3. Her mother *put* the cookies in the oven. (A)

4. The walls of the room *felt* extremely damp. (L)

5. Her friends *are* at the front of that line. (S)

6. She *should have been* at school already. (S)

7. The chairman of the committee *seems* very nervous. (L)

8. The group *moved* quietly through the art museum. (A)

9. She *dreamed* about a new car. (A)

10. His extra class *has become* a real burden. (L)

Quiz #4

1. The children *ran* excitedly toward the house. (A)

2. The largest contributor *will be* the overall winner. (L)

3. She *has become* extremely independent. (L)

4. My friends *are* in their seats in the auditorium already. (S)

5. The story *was* in the paper on Sunday. (S)

6. Our dog *chased* the squirrel up the oak tree. (A)

7. All of the players *appeared* tired. (L)

8. We *have studied* very hard for that test. (A)

9. He *will be* in the next round of the competition. (S)

10. That girl on the stage *is* my best friend. (L)

Quiz #5

1. They *will be shopping* for clothes for three hours. (A)

2. She *was* very tired after the performance. (L)

3. You *were* the only girl in that group. (L)

4. Her little brother *was* there for 30 minutes. (S)

5. My friends *will be waiting* in front at two o'clock. (A)

6. They *were* members of the same team. (L)

7.   We *shall be* near the back of the room. (S)

8.   The windows in the old house *rattled* endlessly in the wind. (A)

9.   Your group *is* over by the flagpole. (S)

10.   My brother and I *were hoping* for rain. (A)

Quiz #6

1.   He *will be* in an important tournament on Friday. (S)

2.   She *appeared* tired and weak. (L)

3.   The dog *dashed* across the street after the ball. (A)

4.   My mother *carried* the groceries into the house. (A)

5.   They *will be* at my house in an hour. (S)

6.   My brother *was* very proud of his presentation. (L)

7.   They *should* not *have been* at the party on Friday night. (S)

8.   That man *has been* in the front row at every game. (S)

9.   The new girl *will be* my partner in tennis. (L)

10.   He *sprinted* quickly across the track to the gym. (A)

Quiz #7

1.   She *swims* laps at the pool every morning. (A)

2.   He often *dreamed* of stardom. (A)

3.   They *were* still in the middle of a heated discussion. (S)

4.   The young boy *seems* much happier now. (L)

5.   She *will* soon *be* my sister-in-law. (L)

6.	The large dog *roamed* around the neighborhood. (A)

7.	The boys *will be* at our house later. (S)

8.	My friend *should be* anxious about the news. (L)

9.	They *are* in the first group of contestants. (S)

10.	My house *is* in the middle of the block. (S)

Quiz #8

1.	The whole group *should have been* in line earlier. (S)

2.	This house *seems* cold and empty. (L)

3.	The rain *had stopped* for only two hours. (A)

4.	That woman in the front row *is* my mother's doctor. (L)

5.	My friends *could* not *have been* at the mall. (S)

6.	She often *imagined* a long trip to Europe. (A)

7.	The three men *have pushed* the car out of traffic. (A)

8.	*There *will* always *be* a place for her on the team. (S)

9.	That man *appears* nervous and confused. (L)

10.	The large boxes *were* in our way. (S)

Quiz #9

1.	My brothers *will be walking* to school tomorrow. (A)

2.	Each of the teams *has* three points. (A)

3.	My friends and I *will be* in the classroom. (S)

4.	The new girl at our school *is* an old friend of mine. (L)

5.	We *are riding* our bicycles every day. (A)

6.   All of the groceries *are* in the back seat of the car. (S)

7.   Her brother *will become* the captain of our team. (L)

8.   Why *is* that man *standing* in the middle of the street? (A)

9.   My sister *is* always tired after practice. (L)

10.   Those three girls *were* in my math class. (S)

Quiz #10

1.   He *carried* his books to the table. (A)

2.   She *was* at the mall for the entire day. (S)

3.   The geese *had landed* on the far side of the lake. (A)

4.   *Will* she ever *become* a famous actress? (L)

5.   She carefully *washed* the dishes for her mother. (A)

6.   The little children *were wading* through every puddle. (A)

7.   The streets of the town *were* completely empty. (L)

8.   They *will be* in the very front of the room. (S)

9.   The large dog *has chased* the cat up the tree. (A)

10.   My parents *had* not *arrived* on time. (A)

Quiz #11

1.   The small cat *ran* quickly across the yard. (A)

2.   My sister *has been* in the store for an hour. (S)

3.   The sky over the mountains *looked* dark and stormy. (L)

4.   The group *is* already at our house. (S)

5. My mother *will be* our troop leader. (L)

6. My friend *could have danced* for three more hours. (A)

7. The ball *flew* over the fence into the empty field. (A)

8. My father *is* always on time. (S)

9. She *looked* across the room at her friend. (A)

10. He *might become* the overall champion by tomorrow. (L)

Quiz #12

1. My mother *will drive* us to the mall. (A)

2. My little sister *picked* flowers from the garden. (A)

3. Her parents *were* very excited about their trip to Russia. (L)

4. We *walked* carefully across the muddy field. (A)

5. You *are* always in the way. (S)

6. The food in the oven *smelled* delicious. (L)

7. My father *will be* the chairman of that committee. (L)

8. The girl with all the books *is* in my math class at school. (S)

9. Those new people in line *are* from New York. (S)

10. My brothers *are carrying* the packages into the house. (A)

Quiz #13

1. My sister *parked* the car next to the school. (A)

2. After the test he *became* very tired. (L)

3. The woman on the screen *is* my favorite actress. (L)

4. The track team quickly *has run* around the track three times. (A)

5. Her little sister *will be* in my class next year. (S)

6. The candidate *moved* easily around the large room. (A)

7. All of the students *were* in line for tickets to the game. (S)

8. The cherries on the tree in our yard *looked* ripe. (L)

9. The baby *crawled* across the kitchen floor. (A)

10. A big yellow kite *was* in the sky over our heads. (S)

Quiz #14

1. They *had been moving* furniture for hours. (A)

2. Lately, she *has become* a wonderful friend. (L)

3. The boys *are* usually in the kitchen for snacks. (S)

4. The girls *should have been* in class already. (S)

5. The whole group *followed* the path through the woods. (A)

6. The room *appeared* dark from the outside. (L)

7. He *has stopped* the ball with his mitt. (A)

8. My sister *will be* at the airport at three o'clock. (S)

9. She *will* soon *be* the best player in the group. (L)

10. The beautiful swan *was* near the edge of the lake. (S)

Quiz #15

1.   The young boy *pushed* his sister in the stroller. (A)

2.   He quickly *ran* into the house from the car. (A)

3.   My friend *has become* a very good tennis player. (L)

4.   Their new house *is* near the city park. (S)

5.   My friends *have* already *been* to the movies. (S)

6.   *Has* she *been* a team captain before? (L)

7.   My family *could* not *move* until the last day of the month. (A)

8.   This room *feels* damp and musty. (L)

9.   She often *remembers* her summer in Hawaii. (A)

10. You *are* always at the front of every ticket line. (S)

Quiz #16

1.   He *did* not *appear* too lonely. (L)

2.   *May* we *stop* at the market first? (A)

3.   We *should have been calling* our mothers from school. (A)

4.   The actress *was looking* extremely confident. (L)

5.   *Could*n't you *eat* a piece of her apple pie? (A)

6.   We *are* not near the parking lot. (S)

7.   *Shall* I *open* the package now? (A)

8.   The entire class *was feeling* ill. (L)

9.   My friend *could have been* there also. (S)

10. You *should be* in the next group. (S)

Quiz #17

1. The young boy *slept* through the noise and sirens. (A)

2. The pitcher *was throwing* the ball to the shortstop (A)

3. My friends *were* already in the car. (S)

4. Her older brother *has become* a fine musician. (L)

5. After the win the team *was* very enthusiastic. (L)

6. Nothing *could have prevented* the accident. (A)

7. The young girl in the play *is* my sister. (L)

8. Our group *was* in the center of the room. (S)

9. The small plane *is flying* into a storm. (A)

10. Several boxes *are* by the front door. (S)

Quiz #18

1. The beautiful horse *was trotting* along the fence. (A)

2. The entire building *appeared* empty. (L)

3. Her sister *has* always *been* my friend. (L)

4. The majestic eagle *was* above the steep cliff. (S)

5. My brother *was chosen* the new chairman of the committee. (A)

6. He *should be* in the middle of his test. (S)

7. Her parents *are* on their way. (S)

8. The field of corn *has grown* four feet. (A)

9. Her forehead *feels* very warm to the touch. (L)

10. The young boys *have caught* three butterflies in their nets. (A)

Chapter 14: Verb Tenses

There will be two different types of quizzes in this section, both dealing with the *regular* tenses of verbs. Every verb has six tenses: *present*, *past*, *future*, *present perfect*, *past perfect*, and *future perfect*.

The first series of quizzes will present a verb, a pronoun, and a tense, and the student will respond by writing the correct form of the verb, including the pronoun. The pronoun is important since *I* and *we* take a different helping verb ("shall") in the future tenses than the other pronouns. The answers will show both the correct form of the verb tense and the pronoun.

The second series of quizzes will be sentences in which the students will determine and write the tense of the verb that is being used. Both the verb and the correct tense will be identified. Some verb conjugations will be regular, some irregular. If extra help with verb recognition is required, students can be asked to write the verb in addition to the tense. A chart showing all of the verb tenses and how they are formed would be helpful.

Note: The present and past tenses of any verb consist of only one word. All perfect tenses of a verb contain some form of the verb *to have* and the past participle of the main verb.

Section One

Section One Key: [P]=Past, [F]=Future, [Pr]=Present, [PP]=Past Perfect, [PrP]=Present Perfect, [FP]=Future Perfect

Quiz #1

Use the pronoun *I* for this entire quiz.

1.   start   [PP]   (I had started)

2.   begin   [P]   (I began)

3.   save   [FP]   (I shall have saved)

4.   wash   [Pr]   (I wash)

5.   drive   [PrP]   (I have driven)

6.   request   [F]   (I shall request)

7.   draw   [PrP]   (I have drawn)

8.   quit   [F]   (I shall quit)

9.   take   [PP]   (I had taken)

10. climb   [FP]   (I shall have climbed)

Quiz #2

1.   he   catch   [F]   (he will catch)

2.   they   start   [PrP]   (they have started)

3.   we   carry   [Pr]   (we carry)

4.   I   play   [FP]   (I shall have played)

5.   she   finish   [P]   (she finished)

6.   I   walk   [PP]   (I had walked)

7.   she   cry   [PrP]   (she has cried)

8.   he   return   [Pr]   (he returns)

9.   they   pull   [PP]   (they had pulled)

10. you   compete   [FP]   (you will have competed)

Quiz #3

1.	he	chase	[PrP]	(he has chased)
2.	you	catch	[Pr]	(you catch)
3.	it	spoil	[PP]	(it had spoiled)
4.	they	suggest	[P]	(they suggested)
5.	she	throw	[PrP]	(she has thrown)
6.	I	try	[FP]	(I shall have tried)
7.	we	plant	[PP]	(we had planted)
8.	they	write	[P]	(they wrote)
9.	it	sail	[FP]	(it will have sailed)
10.	you	speak	[F]	(you will speak)

Quiz #4

1.	she	type	[PP]	(she had typed)
2.	they	fish	[P]	(they fished)
3.	I	begin	[FP]	(I shall have begun)
4.	we	join	[Pr]	(we join)
5.	he	watch	[PrP]	(he has watched)
6.	she	complete	[F]	(she will complete)
7.	I	go	[P]	(I went)
8.	you	sell	[PrP]	(you have sold)
9.	he	shout	[PP]	(he had shouted)
10.	I	travel	[F]	(I shall travel)

Quiz #5

1.	he	speak	[PP]	(he had spoken)

173

2.	she	ring	[Pr]	(she rings)
3.	I	write	[FP]	(I shall have written)
4.	you	know	[PrP]	(you have known)
5.	we	slip	[P]	(we slipped)
6.	she	study	[F]	(she will study)
7.	we	learn	[PrP]	(we have learned)
8.	he	coach	[FP]	(he will have coached)
9.	I	drive	[PP]	(I had driven)
10.	you	collect	[P]	(you collected)

Quiz #6

1.	he	claim	[PrP]	(he has claimed)
2.	I	play	[F]	(I shall play)
3.	we	organize	[PP]	(we had organized)
4.	you	challenge	[FP]	(you will have challenged)
5.	she	carry	[Pr]	(she carries)
6.	it	follow	[P]	(it followed)
7.	we	see	[FP]	(we shall have seen)
8.	I	show	[PP]	(I had shown)
9.	he	add	[P]	(he added)
10.	you	jump	[PrP]	(you have jumped)

Quiz #7

1.	I	push	[FP]	(I shall have pushed)
2.	she	struggle	[Pr]	(she struggles)
3.	you	move	[PrP]	(you have moved)

174

4.	we	report	[PP]	(we had reported)
5.	I	eat	[P]	(I ate)
6.	he	go	[PrP]	(he has gone)
7.	they	hear	[P]	(they heard)
8.	she	make	[PP]	(she had made)
9.	I	trade	[F]	(I shall trade)
10.	he	mail	[FP]	(he will have mailed)

Quiz #8

1.	she	look	[PrP]	(she has looked)
2.	I	swim	[FP]	(I shall have swum)
3	he	present	[P]	(he presented)
4.	you	pull	[F]	(you will pull)
5.	we	sort	[PP]	(we had sorted)
6.	they	sing	[Pr]	(they sing)
7.	you	live	[FP]	(you will have lived)
8.	I	go	[P]	(I went)
9.	he	mail	[PrP]	(he has mailed)
10.	we	develop	[PP]	(we had developed)

Quiz #9

1.	he	stall	[PrP]	(he has stalled)
2.	I	whisper	[Pr]	(I whisper)
3.	we	send	[FP]	(we shall have sent)
4.	they	add	[P]	(they added)
5.	she	perform	[F]	(she will perform)

6.	you	use	[PrP]	(you have used)
7.	she	grow	[PP]	(she had grown)
8.	he	read	[Pr]	(he reads)
9.	you	dress	[FP]	(you will have dressed)
10.	they	fly	[PP]	(they had flown)

Quiz #10

Use the pronoun "he" for this entire quiz.

1.	allow	[PrP]	(he has allowed)
2.	wish	[F]	(he will wish)
3.	yell	[P]	(he yelled)
4.	trade	[Pr]	(he trades)
5.	bring	[FP]	(he will have brought)
6.	arrive	[PP]	(he had arrived)
7.	finish	[Pr]	(he finishes)
8.	sing	[FP]	(he will have sung)
9.	order	[PP]	(he had ordered)
10.	plow	[PrP]	(he has plowed)

Quiz #11

1.	he	stand	[PrP]	(he has stood)
2.	she	close	[P]	(she closed)
3.	we	furnish	[FP]	(we shall have furnished)
4.	they	dance	[PP]	(they had danced)
5.	it	approach	[Pr]	(it approaches)

6.   you   prepare   [PrP]   (you have prepared)

7.   she   float   [P]   (she floated)

8.   I   buy   [F]   (I shall buy)

9.   he   sell   [PP]   (he had sold)

10.   you   dress   [FP]   (you will have dressed)

Quiz #12

1.   he   play   [PrP]   (he has played)

2.   they   wait   [F]   (they will wait)

3.   I   complain   [P]   (I complained)

4.   she   capture   [Pr]   (she captures)

5.   you   talk   [PP]   (you had talked)

6.   I   protect   [FP]   (I shall have protected)

7.   we   relax   [PrP]   (we have relaxed)

8.   he   direct   [Pr]   (he directs)

9.   they   recognize   [PP]   (they had recognized)

10.   you   look   [P]   (you looked)

Quiz #13

1.   he   continue   [PrP]   (he has continued)

2.   I   smile   [F]   (I shall smile)

3.   it   fall   [PP]   (it had fallen)

4.   you   repair   [FP]   (you will have repaired)

5.   we   live   [P]   (we lived)

6.   they   tie   [PrP]   (they have tied)

7.   she   know   [Pr]   (she knows)

177

8.	we	ride	[FP]	(we shall have ridden)
9.	he	focus	[PP]	(he had focused)
10.	they	turn	[P]	(they turned)

Quiz #14

1.	he	choose	[PP]	(he had chosen)
2.	I	hunt	[F]	(I shall hunt)
3.	you	write	[P]	(you wrote)
4.	she	build	[PrP]	(she has built)
5.	they	touch	[FP]	(they will have touched)
6.	it	print	[Pr]	(it prints)
7.	she	sit	[PP]	(she had sat)
8.	I	hike	[FP]	(I shall have hiked)
9.	he	drink	[P]	(he drank)
10.	they	worry	[PrP]	(they have worried)

Quiz #15

1.	it	make	[PP]	(it had made)
2.	I	carry	[FP]	(I shall have carried)
3.	she	dream	[Pr]	(she dreams)
4.	you	return	[PrP]	(you have returned)
5.	they	erase	[P]	(they erased)
6.	we	pass	[F]	(we shall pass)
7.	she	go	[PP]	(she had gone)
8.	they	flash	[FP]	(they will have flashed)
9.	he	fly	[PrP]	(he has flown)

10. I   sort   [P]   (I sorted)

Quiz #16

1.   he   throw   [PP] (he had thrown)

2.   I   select   [F]   (I shall select)

3.   she   surround [Pr] (she surrounds)

4.   we   study   [PrP] (we have studied)

5.   you   prepare   [P]   (you prepared)

6.   they sell   [PP] (they had sold)

7.   she   plan   [FP] (she will have planned)

8.   they fill   [Pr] (they fill)

9.   he   manage   [PrP] (he has managed)

10. we   land   [FP] (we shall have landed)

Quiz #17

Use the pronoun "she" for this entire quiz.

1.   scream   [PP]   (she had screamed)

2.   laugh   [F]   (she will laugh)

3.   follow   [Pr]   (she follows)

4.   win   [FP]   (she will have won)

5.   print   [P]   (she printed)

6.   eat   [PrP]   (she has eaten)

7.   watch   [Pr]   (she watches)

8.   stomp   [FP]   (she will have stomped)

9.   try   [Pr]   (she tries)

10.   drive   [PP]   (she had driven)

Section Two

Quiz #1

1.   My sister *has* always *walked* home from school. (PrP)

2.   He *closed* the kitchen door softly. (P)

3.   I *shall* never *volunteer* for that committee. (F)

4.   *Had* he *brought* in all the groceries? (PP)

5.   *Have* you *had* enough fun for one day? (PrP)

6.   That document *requires* your signature. (Pr)

7.   We *shall have been* in line for three hours. (FP)

8.   My brother *had* recently *returned* from college. (PP)

9.   He easily *swam* the last lap of the relay. (P)

10.   *Will* the last event *have finished* by noon? (FP)

Quiz #2

1.   The chairman of the committee *had chosen* a winner. (PP)

2.   The girl on the stage *looks* exactly like my friend. (Pr)

3.   We *shall see* you in the morning. (F)

4.   My friend *has* already *arrived* at my house. (PrP)

5.   She *walked* a mile to the bus stop. (P)

6.   All of them *will have left* by two o'clock. (FP)

7.   The store owner *has returned* from lunch. (PrP)

8.   The accident on the freeway *had delayed* all traffic. (PP)

9.   We *watched* the entire game. (P)

10. That group *will finish* the project by noon. (F)

Quiz #3

1.   By this evening he *will have played* three matches. (FP)

2.   The speaker *has* already *shown* all of his slides. (PrP)

3.   *Had* the main event of the day *started* by noon? (PP)

4.   My sister *sews* her own costumes for recitals. (Pr)

5.   *Have* all of the campers *brought* warm clothing? (PrP)

6.   We *shall* now *continue* without further interruption. (F)

7.   My friends easily *ran* the last quarter mile. (P)

8.   *Will* the rain ever *stop*? (F)

9.   He *had* already *carried* many boxes to the car. (PP)

10. By the end we *shall have collected* enough for everyone. (FP)

Quiz #4

1.   *Will* they *have sent* the letters by the end of the week? (FP)

181

2. She only *stayed* through the first act. (P)

3. We *have bought* all of the books on the subject. (PrP)

4. They *want* pizza for their party on Friday. (Pr)

5. The boys *had finished* their work at the library. (PP)

6. I *shall return* to the office for the meeting. (F)

7. He *threw* the ball to the shortstop. (P)

8. The telephone *has rung* four times this evening. (PrP)

9. He *will* not *have completed* the project by four o'clock. (FP)

10. My sister *had* never *read* for two hours at one time. (PP)

Quiz #5

1. He *showed* his homework to the teacher. (P)

2. She *will have wandered* around for hours. (FP)

3. They *have* always *delivered* the milk to school. (PrP)

4. The actor *walks* quietly off stage. (Pr)

5. I *shall be* grateful to you forever. (F)

6. All of them *had arrived* at the entrance together. (PP)

7. They *concluded* the program at eight. (P)

8. My family usually *travels* to the lake during the summer. (Pr)

9. He *has* already *announced* the team members. (PrP)

10. The man *had run* out of the house quickly. (PP)

Quiz #6

1. We *have had* beautiful weather all week. (PrP)

2. *Will* they *have arrived* at the station by five? (FP)

3. He *plays* a clarinet in the school band. (Pr)

4. The delicate plants *had frozen* during the night. (PP)

5. He *stopped* the bus at the corner. (P)

6. The woman *has removed* her name from the ballot. (PrP)

7. We *shall leave* early in the morning. (F)

8. The bacon *sizzles* in the pan. (Pr)

9. By evening they *had returned* to the house. (PP)

10. My friend *will* already *have started* her speech by that time. (FP)

Quiz #7

1. The man *has called* three customers to the counter. (PrP)

2. She often *talks* in her sleep. (Pr)

3. They *will have walked* for three hours. (FP)

4. My mother happily *stopped* the car in front of the house. (P)

5. He *had returned* all of the books to the library. (PP)

6. I *shall* probably *arrive* after them. (F)

7. Our neighbor's dog *has run* into the yard. (PrP)

8. She *spoke* very loudly into the microphone. (P)

9. They *will erase* most of those lines. (F)

10. I *had* already *telephoned* from school. (PP)

Quiz #8

1. They *danced* throughout the night. (P)

2. That group of girls *will have won* four different awards. (FP)

3. I *shall apply* for a new license tomorrow. (F)

4. She *smiles* all the time. (Pr)

5. The work on our house *has stopped* for the day. (PrP)

6. The team from the other school *played* three games. (P)

7. He *had* already *begun* his speech to the players. (PP)

8. The teams *have chosen* new captains. (PrP)

9. No one *will remember* all the names on the list. (F)

10. We *shall have competed* by three o'clock on Saturday. (FP)

Quiz #9

1. They *have finished* a wonderful vacation to Europe. (PrP)

2. My friend *returned* home yesterday. (P)

3. I *shall start* my new job on Monday. (F)

4. My sister *runs* three miles every day. (Pr)

5. The rain *will have stopped* by noon. (FP)

6. My father *had* never *worked* late before. (PP)

7. He *has* already *entered* almost every race this year. (PrP)

8. Her sisters *will* not *arrive* for the concert. (F)

9. The small bird *flew* across the yard. (P)

10. The coach *had* soon *called* all of the members of the team. (PP)

Quiz #10

1. We always *play* softball on Sunday. (Pr)

2. She *has* just *completed* all of her chores. (PrP)

3. Nothing *will* ever *change* their minds. (F)

4. My mother *had brought* snacks for the team. (PP)

5. The whole group *came* through the front door together. (P)

6. We *shall* never *forget* our favorite event. (F)

7. My friends *have* really *studied* hard for the test. (PrP)

8. *Had* the firemen *burned* the lady's books? (PP)

9. They *will* probably *have started* by three o'clock. (FP)

10. The couple *strolled* quietly through the park. (P)

Quiz #11

1. We *shall have completed* three projects by five o'clock. (FP)

2. The boys *wanted* sandwiches from the delicatessen. (P)

3. *Have* you *finished* all of the dinner dishes? (PrP)

4. They *will* probably *begin* early in the morning. (F)

5. My little sister *has watched* that movie three times. (PrP)

6. No one *had* ever *seen* her whole performance. (PP)

7. My brother *needs* new shoes for school. (Pr)

8. The stray baseball *broke* a window in our kitchen. (P)

9. *Will* they *have started* by the early afternoon? (FP)

10. He *had chosen* a perfect picnic spot. (PP)

Quiz #12

1. By the end of the week, she *will have brought* three boxes. (FP)

2. The dog *has lain* awake all night on the porch. (PrP)

3. I *shall go* with you in the morning. (F)

4. That lady *paints* for the gallery every day. (Pr)

5. No one *had finished* the story by noon. (PP)

6. That channel *will show* all of the old movies. (F)

7. The dog *performed* tricks for the audience of children. (P)

8. That door *has* always *closed* by itself. (PrP)

9. We *shall have arrived* in the city by late afternoon. (FP)

10. She *screamed* at the top of her lungs. (P)

Quiz #13

1. They *had seen* seven movies in the last week. (PP)

2. He *has shown* his whole collection to them. (PrP)

3. They *will have left* the field by twelve o'clock. (FP)

4. Their parents *stopped* quickly at the mall. (P)

5. The pitcher *throws* the baseball very well. (Pr)

6. I *shall be* a candidate again next time. (F)

7. He *has walked* into that store every day at this time. (PrP)

8. He *will go* with us to the football game. (F)

9. You *will have started* your game by that time. (FP)

10. He *captured* the enemy very quickly. (P)

Quiz #14

1. They *will* not *have gone* to the theater by that time. (FP)

2. The little children *had had* three vacation days. (PP)

3. She *swims* laps in her pool every morning. (Pr)

4. We *have* already *run* two miles around the track. (PrP)

5. *Shall* we *return* a day early? (F)

6. The girls *finished* their practice on time. (P)

7. That student *has* never *asked* a bad question. (PrP)

8. The wind *blew* fiercely all night. (P)

9. No one *had given* them a chance. (PP)

10. They *will* soon *find* the answers to the questions. (F)

Quiz #15

1. We *shall have left* before the final game of the event. (FP)

2. She *runs* in the park each afternoon. (Pr)

3. That boy *has* never *been* to the new mall. (PrP)

4. No one *had thought* of that before. (PP)

5. We *had* never *imagined* so much rain. (PP)

6.   The doctor *has seen* those new patients already. (PrP)

7.   The group *is* not there. (Pr)

8.   The young man *played* basketball for three hours. (P)

9.   The performance *will have stopped* by that time. (FP)

10.   The catcher *has* really *thrown* that ball hard. (PrP)

Quiz #16

1.   I *shall finish* the project soon. (F)

2.   The team easily *broke* the old record. (P)

3.   She *has* never *returned* it on time before. (PrP)

4.   My sister *carries* her own bags on every trip. (Pr)

5.   The car *had* previously *stopped* at another house. (PP)

6.   The candidate *will have called* everyone by this evening. (FP)

7.   *Has* the bell for class already *rung*? (PrP)

8.   The stack of papers *blew* across the grass. (P)

9.   The small child *had* suddenly *run* out of energy. (PP)

10.   The rain *will* surely *pass* quickly. (F)

Quiz #17

1.   The workers *have completed* the entire yard. (PrP)

2.   The family *visited* many museums on vacation. (P)

3.   *Shall* I *return* these books now? (F)

4.   The man *had called* them four different times. (PP)

5.   By tomorrow we *shall have seen* four new colleges. (FP)

6.   My brother always *carries* the groceries from the car. (Pr)

7.   He *will prepare* for the test all week. (F)

8.   *Has* she *ridden* her bike to school? (PrP)

9.   The pitcher *threw* the ball over his head. (P)

10. *Will* they *have finished* by dinner time? (FP)

Quiz #18

1.   *Has* the orchestra *stopped* its rehearsal? (PrP)

2.   My brother *will* never *find* us in the crowd. (F)

3.   Our friend *went* back to college last night. (P)

4.   *Had* the first group of volunteers *finished* by noon? (PP)

5.   Her baby brother *cries* all night long. (Pr)

6.   We *shall* easily *have arrived* by lunchtime. (FP)

7.   The man *had* never *heard* of our governor. (PP)

8.   Until Saturday she *will* not *have competed* in a single event. (FP)

9.   *Have* the judges *made* their choices? (PrP)

10. No one *will win* with that attitude. (F)

Quiz #19

1.   He *has lain* awake for three hours. (PrP)

2.   They *watched* the television program closely. (P)

3.   The wind *will have stopped* by game time. (FP)

189

4.   It *had rained* all night long. (PP)

5.   My brother *has* soup every day for lunch. (Pr)

6.   No one *will see* him behind the stage. (F)

7.   He *laid* his overcoat across the chair. (P)

8.   The president *has spoken* to the club members. (PrP)

9.   We *shall have competed* by this time tomorrow. (FP)

10. Many of the guests *had* already *left* the hall. (PP)

Quiz #20

1.   My friend *has taken* a later bus. (PrP)

2.   I *shall* not *continue* this project next week. (F)

3.   My brother and his friends *walk* to school every day. (Pr)

4.   *Had* the team *come* to the party by eight o'clock? (PP)

5.   We *brought* refreshments for the party. (P)

6.   *Have* the others in our group already *finished* their jobs? (PrP)

7.   The tour group *had* never *seen* the Statue of Liberty. (PP)

8.   *Will* they *have completed* the repairs by the end of the week? (FP)

9.   He anxiously *drove* around the block. (P)

10. You *will learn* about many countries and cultures. (F)

Chapter 15: Active Voice, Passive Voice

Whenever possible, students should write in active voice, where the subject of the sentence is performing the action. With a passive voice verb, the action is "done to" the subject by someone or something else. A passive voice verb will always contain some form of the verb "to be." Both active and passive voice verbs can be written in any of the six tenses.

In the following quizzes, students will determine whether the verbs are written in the active or passive voice. The verb will be in italics in each sentence, and the voice will follow in parentheses. Students will write "A" for Active or "P" for Passive. For extra practice students can also write the verb.

Quiz #1

1. The young boy *chased* the ball. (A)

2. The windows *had been washed* by the handyman. (P)

3. I *shall sing* that song again at the assembly. (A)

4. The small fire *has been extinguished* by the firemen. (P)

5. My best friend *runs* three miles every morning. (A)

6. The supplies *will have been bought* by the committee before noon. (P)

7. The wagon *was pulled* by two beautiful horses. (P)

8. My friend *takes* pictures on every trip. (A)

9. She *has kept* all of the pictures. (A)

10. The new car *had been washed* by the young man. (P)

Quiz #2

1. The small ball *rolled* under the car. (A)
2. The play *was presented* by my drama class. (P)
3. A goal *will be scored* soon by our team. (P)
4. The young man *has received* a wonderful award. (A)
5. The floor *had been swept* from top to bottom. (P)
6. The race *will be run* by both teams. (P)
7. The rose *blossomed* on the vine by the fence. (A)
8. That song *has been sung* by a new group. (P)
9. Dark clouds *raced* across the sky. (A)
10. That movie *was filmed* in New York City. (P)

Quiz #3

1. Her hair *was blown* by the wind. (P)
2. Her brother *plays* the clarinet in the school band. (A)
3. My mother *had baked* enough cookies for the whole class. (A)
4. Our car *will have been returned* by the mechanic by Friday. (P)
5. The school lunches *are delivered* by her every day. (P)
6. *Shall* I *return* your books tomorrow? (A)
7. *Has* the lawn *been mowed* yet by the gardener? (P)
8. The customer *chewed* the tough steak patiently. (A)

9. She *has selected* the new students for the project. (A)

10. A delicious lunch *had been prepared* by the chef. (P)

Quiz #4

1. The fly ball *sailed* over the high wall at the back of the field. (A)

2. A detailed map *was reviewed* by the hikers. (P)

3. Two children *were dropped* off by their parents. (P)

4. They *had been sent* to buy more soda for the dance. (P)

5. A tiny puppy *slept* in a basket by the fire. (A)

6. Several students *order* new uniforms each year. (A)

7. All the bicycles *have been parked* near the fence by the students. (P)

8. The bulletin *is* now *read* at the beginning of each day. (P)

9. School supplies *are purchased* by all the parents. (P)

10. We *shall* all *have finished* lunch by 1:30. (A)

Quiz #5

1. Many products *are marketed* by movie stars. (P)

2. My friends and I *have swum* laps every day this week. (A)

3. *Will* the time for the performance *be changed?* (P)

4. The telephone *rang* very early this morning. (A)

5. Colorful papers *had been stacked* on the table. (P)

6. Those scientists *have invented* a new product. (A)

7. My parents *arrived* at school by 3 o'clock. (A)

8. Several senators *have been reelected* already. (P)

9. Those packages *will* not *be sent* until Friday. (P)

10. The catcher always *throws* to the second baseman. (A)

Quiz #6

1. My best friend *gave* us a ride home after the game. (A)

2. The concert *was sponsored* by Pepsi. (P)

3. Six students *have been enrolled* in the program. (P)

4. The television broadcast *provided* very unpleasant news. (A)

5. Everyone *believes* in ghosts on Halloween. (A)

6. All of the papers *had been passed* back to the students. (P)

7. The awards *were presented* by the club's president. (P)

8. They *will arrive* at the party after us. (A)

9. The books *had been returned* on time. (P)

10. Several products *will be tested* by our consumer committee. (P)

Quiz #7

1. The gardener *planted* orchids along the back wall. (A)

2. The dried leaves *were scattered* by the wind. (P)

3. My mother *will take* a photograph of the whole team. (A)

4. A tall soda *had been placed* on the counter by the door. (P)

5. *Will* the rough road *be repaired* this weekend? (P)

6. The dentist *filled* several of the young man's teeth. (A)

7. Elections *have* already *been held* for the three fulltime positions. (P)

8. The large sheet of paper *was blown* across the yard. (P)

9. His place in the play *will be taken* by his best friend. (P)

10. I *shall return* the library books on time. (A)

Quiz #8

1. Without his tools the carpenter *had done* no work. (A)

2. The football team *performed* very well at Friday's game. (A)

3. Several new lamps *have been bought* from that store. (P)

4. Her car *will have been driven* over 1000 miles by the weekend. (P)

5. The expert *has restored* all the broken pieces. (A)

6. The junior choir *has sung* at many locations this season. (A)

7. Three softball games *had been played* that day. (P)

8. That girl *was chosen* over the others her age. (P)

9. The track *is run* every morning by the whole team. (P)

10. *Was* her paper *graded* by others in the class? (P)

Section IV: ADJECTIVES

Chapter 16: Recognizing Adjectives

The quizzes that follow will test the students' knowledge of adjectives, whether they appear in front of a noun, at the beginning of the sentence, or after a linking verb as a predicate adjective. All types of adjectives, including proper, demonstrative, pronominal, interrogative, indefinite, possessive, and descriptive, will appear in the quizzes. An adjective answers *which one*, *what kind*, or *how many*, and any word with an apostrophe "s" (other than a contraction) will always be an adjective.

In these quizzes adjectives, (minus articles), will be in italics, and the number of adjectives in the sentence will appear in parentheses at the end of each. Students should write all the adjectives.

Note: Do not include the articles "a," "an," and "the" since these three words are always adjectives.

Quiz #1

1. *Beautiful*, the *blue* ocean rolled up on the *soft*, *white* sand. (4)

2. The *new light* bulb was very *bright*. (3)

3. *This* book is *due* at the *corner* library. (3)

4. *Her small* bedroom was *cheery* and *sunny*. (4)

5. A *tiny*, *yellow* butterfly landed on the *thin tree* branch. (4)

6. *Shiny*, *his gold* ring lay at the bottom of the *deep* pool. (4)

7. *That messy* space is *my brother's* locker. (4)

8. *Their* friends were *surprised* at *her good* news. (4)

9. *Many tired* athletes walked around the *large* track. (3)

10. The *steep* trail was *muddy* and very *slippery*. (3)

Quiz #2

1. *His father's* car was parked in the *school parking* lot. (4)

2. The *Chinese* food tasted extremely *spicy*. (2)

3. *Several antique* lamps were purchased at the *local flea* market. (4)

4. *John's* friends are meeting the *other team* members at the *bowling* alley. (4)

5. *That long* road leads to the top of the *highest* peak. (3)

6. *Numerous*, the *math* problems on the *standardized* test were *difficult*. (4)

7. The *large* gym was *quiet* and *empty*. (3)

8. *Our American* flag is *red*, *white*, and *blue*. (5)

9. *My mother's delicious* brownies were on the *kitchen* counter. (4)

10. *Nervous*, the *next* contestants waited in a *long* line. (3)

Quiz #3

1. The *young* man was extremely *happy* with *his new* calculator. (4)

2. She will try *every* key in *that* lock. (2)

3. On the *long kitchen* table lay *three* baskets of *colored* eggs. (4)

4. *My next piano* lesson will be on *Thursday* evening. (4)

5. *Her* very *difficult* test took *three* hours. (3)

6. *His* friend was *excited* but also *nervous* and *anxious*. (4)

7. *This evening's* performance will be *special*. (3)

8. Across the *clear blue* sky flew *several colorful* kites. (4)

9. *Each* box contained *specific* props for *that afternoon's* event. (4)

10. *Their last* assignment covered *old* material from *two* chapters. (4)

Quiz #4

1. Very *proud*, the *small* boy accepted *his* award. (3)

2. *One* day *my best* friend will be *famous*. (4)

3. The *tall pine* trees swayed in the *strong* wind. (3)

4. *My* mother placed a *beautiful* bouquet on the *coffee* table. (3)

5. There was too *much* junk in *his school* locker. (3)

6. A *shiny, new* car pulled into the *theater parking* lot. (4)

7. *Both* boys were very *nervous* about *their upcoming* audition. (4)

8. *This* book is about a *young* girl in a *new* country. (3)

9. *Tom's* father noticed *several* mistakes in *his son's* paper. (4)

10. *Happy, his sister's* friend joined us at the *track* meet. (4)

Quiz #5

1.   *My little* sister has been very *sick.* (3)

2.   *Her* friends preferred the *comfortable* sofa. (2)

3.   *Their Sunday* barbecue was at the *city* park. (3)

4.   *His full* backpack was *heavy,* and the strap was *broken.* (4)

5.   *Quiet,* the *small* child sat in the *dark, unoccupied* room. (4)

6.   *That old* book on the *top* shelf is extremely *valuable.* (4)

7.   On *Friday* night *my* brother attended *his tenth college* reunion. (5)

8.   There is nothing *better* than *cold* water on a *hot* day. (3)

9.   *My sister's science* test was *difficult,* but she received a *good* grade. (5)

10. You will need *scratch* paper, a *sharp* pencil, and *this* calculator for *your algebra* test. (5)

Quiz #6

1.   The *three* children had found a very *large* cave in the *nearby* mountain. (3)

2.   *My good* friend was terribly *excited* about *her* chances in the *next* race. (5)

3.   They carried bowls of *mashed* potatoes, *turkey* stuffing, and *cranberry* sauce to *each* table. (4)

4.   *My little* sister played on the *outdoor* equipment. (3)

5.   *That particular* author writes *wonderful mystery* stories. (4)

6. He closed *his* eyes and imagined a *new* bicycle in a *beautiful blue* color. (4)

7. A *special* menu was provided for the *evening* banquet. (2)

8. *Six* members of the *softball* team brought *their* friends to the game. (3)

9. *This* pile of *construction* paper will be used for *our science* project. (4)

10. The *young* woman felt *secure* in *her recent job* interview. (5)

Quiz #7

1. A *big brown* bear stood near the *large trash* pile. (4)

2. The *old* man put on a *ragged, gray* coat and *torn* gloves. (4)

3. The *noble* prince banished *fair* Romeo from *his* city. (3)

4. *My beautiful* roses brightened the *dark, gloomy* room. (4)

5. *Thrilled, my* mother listened carefully to the *morning* news. (3)

6. *Her new* announcement made a *big* impression on the *restless* crowd. (4)

7. *Three large* jumps had been set up on the *old obstacle* course. (4)

8. The *new* student was *tall* and extremely *intelligent*. (3)

9. The *dim* light from the *mansion's* library could be seen from the *empty* hall. (3)

10. A *bright shooting* star flashed across the *clear, dark, summer* sky. (5)

Quiz #8

1. The *small* child was very *brave* during *his solo* performance. (4)

2. They will always bring *special* souvenirs from *their many* excursions. (3)

3. *That last* problem on *our* homework was *tricky*. (4)

4. The *beautiful* weather will continue for *Patricia's outdoor* wedding. (3)

5. By *New York* standards *city* living here is relatively *inexpensive*. (3)

6. *His shiny red* wagon was parked by the *kitchen* door. (4)

7. The *excited* but *nervous* contestants waited behind the *closed* door. (3)

8. *Four* members of the *soccer* team won *blue* ribbons. (3)

9. *Those* answers were *easy*. (2)

10. *My good* friend wanted to use *our swimming* pool for *her birthday* party. (6)

Quiz #9

1. The *three* girls walked very quickly through the *narrow, dark* alley. (3)

2. *My* sister brought *her* friends to *our special* concert. (4)

3. We read *that particular* book in the *fifth* grade. (3)

4. The *boy's bright* eyes became *enormous* as he noticed *his* gift. (4)

5. *Elegant*, the costumes for the *formal* event were very *expensive*. (3)

6. A *shiny new* penny was found on the *wet* concrete. (3)

7. *Her* friend is a *famous* actress and *television* star. (3)

8. *Their* classmates brought them *chocolate* malts from the *nearby soda* shop. (4)

9. The *anxious* parents awaited the *final* performance and presentation of *achievement* awards. (3)

10. The *remaining* contestants were extremely *anxious* in the *back* corner of the *large* auditorium. (4)

Quiz #10

1. The *tall, green* grass was *damp* with *morning* dew. (4)

2. A *final* contestant took *his* place on the *starting* line. (3)

3. *My* mother was *pleased* with *every* display at the *large* exhibit. (4)

4. *That last* question on *our history* test was *difficult* and *confusing*. (6)

5. *Those heavy* rains soaked the *window* screens and *our patio* furniture. (5)

6. *Many plastic* cups and *paper* plates will be bought for *Saturday's* event. (4)

7. *This mountain* village is the *perfect vacation* spot. (4)

8. *Blue* and *red* folders contained the *important* information. (3)

9. The *fluffy, white* kittens in the *store* window were *adorable.* (4)

10. *Loud* thunder rumbled endlessly across the *gloomy, gray* sky. (3)

Quiz #11

1. A *small, square* box lay on the *top* shelf of the *kitchen* pantry. (4)

2. *Her* brother was really *pleased* with *his new* job. (4)

3. *That large* pile of *fallen* leaves needs to go in *Friday's* trash. (4)

4. *Many colorful* paintings lined the *gallery* walls. (3)

5. *His beautiful, new* car was parked in front of the *local* theater. (4)

6. The leaves on the ground were *yellow, red,* and *orange.* (3)

7. *My little* sister is always *happy* at *her summer* camp. (5)

8. *Blue, red,* and *white satin* ribbons were awarded at the *track* meet. (5)

9. *These green* markers belong in the *prize* booth by the *farthest* entrance. (4)

10. *Their* friends were *eager* participants in the *alumni baseball* game. (4)

Quiz #12

1. A *clear, blue* sky greeted the *morning* sun. (3)

2. He had a very *large* bump on *his* forehead from the *accidental* meeting with the *bedroom* door. (4)

3. We were *unhappy* with the *bright pastel* colors of the *kitchen* wall. (4)

4. A *big rubber* raft floated peacefully with the *river's gentle* current. (4)

5. *Three hard* tests were scheduled for *that* day, but we were *ready*. (4)

6. A *steady* line of cars blocked the *main* entrance to the *county* fair. (3)

7. It is extremely *difficult* to write a *clever* and *imaginative* story. (3)

8. *This large* blanket will provide *great* warmth in the *cold* weather. (4)

9. *Six bright neon* lights were hanging from *my garage* ceiling. (5)

10. The *curious, little* cat poked *her black* nose into the *large* bucket of *white* paint. (6)

Quiz #13

1. The *young* boy walked through the *large, crowded* store. (3)

2. The *American* ballerina was *graceful* and *beautiful*. (3)

3. *Our last baseball* game of *this* season will be played on *Monday* night. (5)

4. We went to a *fancy* restaurant for *delicious Chinese* food. (3)

5. *His new, red* bicycle was borrowed by *my best* friend. (5)

6. *Their dusty library* books sat on an *elegant antique* table in the *dark* parlor. (6)

7. *Those* toys belong on the *proper* shelf in *your bedroom* closet. (4)

8. The *next* performer seems extremely *talented*. (2)

9. *Every* member of *my* team received a *special* award. (3)

10. An *old* box of *chocolate* candy was discovered on the *bottom* shelf. (3)

Quiz #14

1. The *sad, lonely* child sat in *his* room in the *large, empty* house. (5)

2. The *tiny, white* puppy was *scared* by the *loud* crack of thunder. (4)

3. A *long, windy* trail climbed near the *clear, rushing* stream. (4)

4. They finished the *morning* race and returned to *his* house. (2)

5. A very *large, blue* basket was sitting on the *cluttered* counter. (3)

6. *Our Saturday morning* game was moved to a *larger, better* field. (5)

7. We were *upset* with the *final* results of the *junior art* contest. (4)

8. The *young* girl called *her best* friend to get the *latest homework* assignment. (5)

9. A *huge* pile of *old* magazines was occupying the *office storage* shelves. (4)

10. *Bright* lights shone from *her upstairs bedroom* window. (4)

Quiz #15

1. The *small, happy* boy appeared *tired*. (3)

2. There was a *large red* robin in the *oak* tree outside *my* window. (4)

3. *That young* man was *careless* and *irresponsible*. (4)

4. A *huge* wall of *muddy* water rushed down the *dark* canyon. (3)

5. *Our new* neighbor has *three small* children and *two* dogs. (5)

6. The *afternoon* forecast was *dark* and *dreary*. (3)

7. We shall have a *track* meet on *Saturday* afternoon. (2)

8. *Your June* weather is usually quite *pleasant*. (3)

9. He looked *handsome* in *his new* suit and *fashionable* tie. (4)

10. The *blue* sky contained *some white, fluffy* clouds. (4)

Quiz #16

1. *Curious*, the *small, brown* dog ran circles around the *large* yard. (4)

2. He was extremely *tired* from *his long* day at the *chess* tournament. (4)

3. The *clear, blue* sky was suddenly filled with a *great* flock of *Canadian* geese. (4)

4. *Many* students entered the *state speech* contest to win *college* scholarships. (4)

5. A *blue* and *white* van arrived at *our* school on *Friday* morning. (4)

6. The *clean* locker was a *wonderful* example of *that student's* organization. (4)

7. She wore a *yellow* blouse with a *tan* skirt and a very *colorful* scarf. (3)

8. He was *proud* as he accepted the *special* award from *his school's* principal. (4)

9. A *surprise birthday* party is planned for *next* Saturday. (3)

10. The *golden* sun set over the *glistening*, *blue* waves of the Pacific Ocean. (3)

Quiz #17

1. The *sweet* music filled the *fellowship* hall at *our* church. (3)

2. *My* mother baked a *dozen* cookies for *our afternoon* dance. (4)

3. During the *long* race, he became *sore* and *exhausted*. (3)

4. The very *dark* sky warned of *much* rain and *heavy*, *strong* winds. (4)

5. The end of the *steep* trail was a *welcome* sight to the *weary* hikers. (3)

6. She was *beautiful* in *her long*, *blue* gown and *sparkling* jewelry. (5)

7. A *loud* roar came from inside the *packed football* stadium. (3)

8. The *polite* lady held the *heavy* door as *several* people passed through. (3)

9. *My younger* sister has a *history* test *this* afternoon. (4)

10. *Most* students in *our* class had returned *their* *permission* slips. (4)

Quiz #18

1. *That big* book belongs to *my* sister and *her* husband. (4)

2. The *violent* storm destroyed the *unfinished* wing of *our new* school. (4)

3. A *black* and *white* car pulled out of *their neighbor's* driveway. (4)

4. A *brilliant* star shone over the *steep* roof of the *old* mansion. (3)

5. The *two* cartons of milk in the refrigerator were *sour*. (2)

6. *Three brown* kittens lay next to *their* mother in the *large wicker* basket. (5)

7. The *boy's* bicycle was parked near a *shiny, red pickup* truck. (4)

8. She needed a *clean, white* piece of *construction* paper to complete *her final art* project. (6)

9. A *huge* chunk of granite was blocking the *only* road to the *winter ski* resort. (4)

10. They had already seen *four* elephants and *two large* lions on *their morning* tour of the *game* preserve. (6)

Quiz #19

1. The *young* boy was *tired* and *grumpy*. (3)

2. *Every* student had a *clean, blue* cap and a *pressed* uniform. (4)

3. *Huge*, the *cold* drops of rain hit *her* face. (3)

4. A *polished, new* motorcycle was parked at the *corner* house. (3)

5. The answers to *your* questions are written on a *small* piece of *yellow* paper. (3)

6. *Three different* levels of difficulty were presented on the *math* test *last* weekend. (4)

7. A *large granite* boulder lay across the *narrow bridle* path. (4)

8. The *old, gray* horse grazed peacefully in the *large* field. (3)

9. *My closest* friend lives *one* block from *our* school. (4)

10. *Her black* shoes were *shiny*, and the *long* laces were *pink*. (5)

Quiz #20

1. *Her tiny sports* car pulled out of the *steep* driveway. (4)

2. *Seven late library* books were returned on *Saturday* afternoon. (4)

3. The *dark* room had *no* lights. (2)

4. A pile of *dirty* dishes greeted *my* mother *this* morning. (3)

5. She was extremely *nervous* about *her important* presentation. (3)

6. The *red* and *yellow* tulips blossomed in *our* gardener's greenhouse. (4)

7. On *Monday* morning *my whole* family leaves on *our summer* trip. (5)

8. *That Indian* pottery has become very *expensive.* (3)

9. *Her empty* locker was a *welcome* sight at the end of the *school* year. (4)

10. A *heavy* rain had created *large* puddles on the *empty* street. (3)

Quiz #21

1. *Her prom* dress was *lovely*, and *her* parents were so *proud.* (5)

2. The *thick* underbrush protected the *young* fawn from hunters. (2)

3. The very *old* newspaper was *faded* and *torn.* (3)

4. *My younger brother's* band will perform on *Tuesday* night. (4)

5. *Your new* locker is in the *other* building. (3)

6. A *grand buffet* table was set up in *no* time. (3)

7. The *bright* sun rose slowly over the *high, snowy* peaks. (3)

8. *Several* girls brought *pink* and *red* roses for the *dinner* tables. (4)

9. A *shiny, bright* button lay on the *soft, blue* carpet. (4)

10. *Many colorful* posters decorated the *small, empty conference* room. (5)

Quiz #22

1. *His new* car had a *flat* tire. (3)

213

2. A *magnificent* painting hung over the *high* mantel. (2)

3. A *huge* pile of *recycled plastic* bottles caught *her* attention. (4)

4. *My brother's best* friend spent *last* night at *our* house. (5)

5. The *calico* kitten was *curious* about the *new* toy. (3)

6. The *dusty, broken* windows in the *empty* house reflected *no* light. (4)

7. The *baby's sweet* smile placed her in *many television* commercials. (4)

8. *That ancient kerosene* lamp is *priceless*. (4)

9. A very *strong afternoon* wind moved the *patio* furniture around *his* yard. (4)

10. *Careful* instructions accompanied *my father's first* computer. (4)

Quiz #23

1. *Her bright* eyes sparkled in the *sun's* light. (3)

2. *My* mother bought a *French* poodle for *my sister's* birthday. (4)

3. *That art* book belongs to the *public* library. (3)

4. *Large, yellow* leaves appeared on the *tall sycamore* tree in *our* yard. (5)

5. *His little* brother was really *careful* with *that crystal* vase. (5)

6. *Useless, those red* pencils need to be put away. (3)

7. *This beautiful, purple* dress will be the *grand* prize at the *celebrity* auction. (5)

214

8. She was *unhappy* about the *low* grade on *her science* test. (4)

9. A *fancy racing* bicycle was in *his family* room on Christmas. (4)

10. The group seemed *excited* about *its* performance at the *city* park on *Friday* night. (4)

Quiz #24

1. *Eager, his little* sister ran toward the *crowded boarding* area. (5)

2. *Those* members of *my* team were *upset* by the *official* results. (4)

3. *Shredded* paper and *colorful* streamers littered the *empty* street. (3)

4. The *Boston* skyline was *beautiful* in the *evening* light. (3)

5. *Our morning basketball* practice lasted for *two long* hours. (5)

6. *Her new locker* combination was *easy* to remember. (4)

7. *My debate* partner won *first* place in a *local speech* contest. (5)

8. The *difficult homework* assignment contained *new* information. (3)

9. *Their* faces were *damp* from the *salt* spray of the *beautiful, blue* ocean. (5)

10. They were *tired* and *hungry* after *Friday's long* competition. (4)

Quiz #25

1. *My last history* test was extremely *easy.* (4)

2. *Four tiny calico* kittens slept by the *warm* fire. (4)

3. The *slippery* road caused *several serious* accidents. (3)

4. There were *three spotted* owls at the top of *our pine* tree. (4)

5. *My* brother needed *new tennis* shoes and a *lighter* racket for *his* tournament. (5)

6. The *young* child cried loudly as *her* mother left the *crowded* room. (3)

7. The *six remaining* contestants were not even *nervous.* (3)

8. *Her best* friend helped *their* team win the *city soccer* championship. (5)

9. The *heavy* clothes were *damp* from the *constant* rain. (3)

10. *Anxious, my little* sister forgot to close the *front* door. (4)

Quiz #26

1. A *bright* light shone across the *glassy* surface of the *small* lake. (3)

2. The *student* council chose *blue* and *red* streamers for *dance* decorations. (4)

3. *Her* room was very *neat* and *clean.* (3)

4. *Numerous* times *his* mother bought *more* soda. (3)

5. The *high* tower on the *college* campus had *few* windows. (3)

216

6.   *Famous, that* author spoke at *her sister's* school. (4)

7.   The *lovely* weather remained for the *entire* week. (2)

8.   *That last history* class was very *scared* about *their* presentations. (5)

9.   During *this* summer we will enjoy *several national* parks. (3)

10.   *Its sleek, red* coat gleamed in the *August* sun. (4)

Quiz #27

1.   The *little* boy found *his lost* toy and was *happy*. (4)

2.   *My closest* friend is coming to the *new* mall with us. (3)

3.   *Four* books fell to the *wet* ground by the *parked, red* car. (4)

4.   The *large* room was *cold* and *damp*, and she was *scared*. (4)

5.   A *new, yellow* basket sat on the *guest room* table. (4)

6.   *White, fluffy* clouds filled the *April* sky. (3)

7.   *That extra* paper belongs on the *long* table by the *back* door. (4)

8.   *Her oldest* sister bought *those* shoes for her. (3)

9.   The *Saturday afternoon football* game was moved to a *different* stadium. (4)

10.   *Our* house is very *close* to *that new Chinese* restaurant. (5)

Quiz #28

1. A *bright* star shone in the *clear evening* sky. (3)

2. *His* appearance was always *neat* and *tidy*. (3)

3. *Those* *three* books on the *coffee* table are *biographical* stories. (4)

4. *My next* performance will be on *Saturday* night. (3)

5. The *library* books had been *heavy*, but now *her* backpack was *empty*. (4)

6. *Many talented* performers arrived early and were practicing *their* acts. (3)

7. *Pretty, pink* blossoms appeared on the *plum* tree in *our* yard. (4)

8. A *loud* crash came from the *far* end of *this* hallway. (3)

9. *Green* and *yellow* flags flew from the roof of the *tall, downtown office* building. (5)

10. *Her final softball* game will be played on *Friday* afternoon. (4)

Section V: ADVERBS

Chapter 17: Recognizing Adverbs

In the following quizzes, students will practice recognition of adverbs, words that modify *verbs*, *adjectives*, or other *adverbs*. Adverbs answer <u>when</u>, <u>where</u>, and <u>how</u> and can be found anywhere in the sentence. There are certain words that are *always* adverbs (including "always," "almost," "never," "too," "here"), and any word that makes a verb negative is also an adverb. Any word that normally would begin a prepositional phrase but is used by itself in the sentence is also an adverb.

In these quizzes adverbs will appear in italics, and the number of adverbs in the sentence will be shown in parentheses at the end of each. Students should write all adverbs.

Quiz #1

1.   We will *always* arrive *there* on time. (2)

2.   My friend will *not ever* be comfortable *here* in the city. (3)

3.   *Soon* a *very* fine rain was falling *steadily* over the mountains. (3)

4.   You did *not* look *everywhere*. (2)

5.   He *never* returns things *promptly*. (2)

6.   They are *almost home*. (2)

7.   The *extremely* young children were *too* tired to go *on*. (3)

8.   *Tomorrow*, we shall *finally* finish painting the house. (2)

9.   He will go *anywhere* if you ask him *politely*. (2)

10. *Suddenly*, she could *not* see the *really* tall bridge in the fog. (3)

Quiz #2

1. *Yesterday*, we *very quickly* changed the program. (3)
2. He could *never* come *home* for the weekend. (2)
3. They will *always* win this type of race *easily*. (2)
4. *Later*, an *extremely* loud crash was heard. (2)
5. *Usually*, she arrives *quite early*. (3)
6. The *very* dark clouds *nearly* touched the ground. (2)
7. We were *not* allowed *too* much time to prepare. (2)
8. We can *never* arrive *late* for a test at school. (2)
9. She *then* took the three *quite* large boxes to the *already* crowded garage. (3)
10. Do *not* get *up* from the table *so fast*. (4)

Quiz #3

1. We have *already* seen *too* many errors. (2)
2. *Ordinarily*, several *newly* arrived visitors attend the meeting. (2)
3. *Soon*, the *very* small river will become a roaring torrent. (2)
4. They could *never ever* remember his *extremely* long address. (3)
5. *Recently*, a *much too* strong wind blew a cloud of dust over the city. (3)
6. *Often*, my friend has new supplies for school. (1)

7.   She should *not* become *too* confident. (2)

8.   The boy *quickly* turned *around*. (2)

9.   He *carefully* put his costume *on*. (2)

10.   *Tomorrow*, the weather should be *only* *slightly* cooler. (3)

Quiz #4

1.   They were *not too* happy with the *very* sloppy work. (3)

2.   *Instantly*, an *extremely* bright light could *clearly* be seen. (3)

3.   She is *always* ready and *never* complains. (2)

4.   *Yesterday*, we *frantically* searched for our science notes. (2)

5.   *Sometimes*, we *only* play two games. (2)

6.   He could *not* have been *more* excited with the results. (2)

7.   The *most* beautiful vase was *much too* expensive. (3)

8.   The group *surprisingly* became *really* focused before their event. (2)

9.   *Quite quickly*, the boy had *already* begun his *very* difficult performance. (4)

10.   She was *never completely* satisfied with her grade. (2)

Quiz #5

1.   *Very soon* there will *not* be any undeveloped areas. (3)

2. He has *already* chosen a team mascot, *too*. (2)

3. *Usually,* she *really* needs my help. (2)

4. She is *actually so* happy when she comes *home*. (3)

5. They *always* had the *most* beautiful garden. (2)

6. He was *very* excited and *quite easily* won the event. (3)

7. *Suddenly,* he could *not even* locate his friend in the crowd. (3)

8. The peaches were *so overly* ripe they would *never* have made it to the picnic in one piece. (3)

9. The boy *quickly* dashed under the *extremely* low fence and was *already* on his way *home.* (4)

10. *Early* in the morning we *quite often* ride our bikes around the park loop. (3)

Quiz #6

1. They watched *very carefully* but did *not* move *too close.* (5)

2. *Tuesday,* you will *really* need to arrive *early.* (3)

3. *Rather swiftly,* an *extremely* large flock of geese landed on the lake. (3)

4. *So far only* two contestants had *not* checked *in.* (5)

5. The group moved *slowly away* from the final exhibit. (2)

6. My friends were *too* busy *ever* to come for a visit. (2)

7. We *almost always* finish our tests *extremely late.* (4)

8. We will *not soon* be planning another surprise party. (2)

9. *Friday*, many of us will *already* have left. (2)

10. *Sometimes,* we do *not* consider the *most* obvious answer. (3)

Quiz #7

1. A *rather* long train rumbled *slowly* through the *almost* deserted town. (3)

2. If you are *not* on the committee, you have the *least* demanding job. (2)

3. The manager is *always so* pleasant when she is *not too* busy. (4)

4. They could *almost certainly* imagine that he would *mysteriously* appear. (3)

5. *Tonight*, we shall *never* arrive *home* before nine. (3)

6. *Surely*, they have *simply* forgotten the directions. (2)

7. *Thursday*, my friends will arrive *promptly* after school. (2)

8. He was *almost too* tired to compete *really well*. (4)

9. *Now*, the opening will *certainly* be delayed *indefinitely*. (3)

10. *Unfortunately*, they can*not ever* return to that specific location. (3)

Quiz #8

1. The *very* tired athletes returned to the gym *quite slowly*. (3)

2. A *most* wonderful surprise *unexpectedly* awaited them. (2)

3. *Tomorrow*, we will *not* bring *so* many books. (3)

225

4. He had *never really* noticed that they were *frequently* late. (3)

5. *Rather quickly* the music became *too* loud. (3)

6. They could *not easily* criticize the *much* needed help. (3)

7. The young girl was *extremely* pleased with the *very* complimentary note. (2)

8. The group had *already* purchased tickets and programs, *also*. (2)

9. The man has *so kindly* ordered group pictures for us, *too*. (3)

10. *Never before* had she seen *so* many *really* talented performers. (4)

Quiz #9

1. The *quite* unusual story was *always greatly* appreciated by a *slightly* older audience. (4)

2. *Very quietly*, she entered the *almost* deserted auditorium. (3)

3. *Never* lose the *extremely* positive attitude you *already* have. (3)

4. He could *not even* begin the *really* difficult problems. (3)

5. They were *most* anxious to go to the concert, *also*. (2)

6. *Yesterday*, he realized he would *always* be *too* tired to compete *successfully*. (4)

7. My friend was *only slightly* interested in the *rather* unique idea. (3)

8. She *slowly* walked *home* since it was *not yet* dark. (4)

9. *Eagerly*, the *very* young children explored the *nearly* empty amusement park. (3)

10. *Soon*, it would be *too late* to go *home*. (4)

Quiz # 10

1. *Too quickly*, the *terribly* exciting trip was *nearly* finished. (4)

2. *Soon*, the *rather* gray clouds moved *in* from the mountains. (3)

3. He could *already* see the tops of the *not too* tall trees. (3)

4. *Saturday*, my parents will *most likely* return about noon. (3)

5. The committee was *more* disappointed by the *extremely* poor turnout. (2)

6. She had *never really* been *so* involved in a project *before*. (4)

7. *Accidentally*, a *very* large piece of scaffolding fell from *overhead*. (3)

8. My mother was *not completely* certain that she had *thoroughly* answered the questions. (3)

9. We shall *quite easily* arrive *home tomorrow*. (4)

10. *Later*, they will *probably* be *so* tired they will *not* care. (4)

Quiz #11

1. *Yesterday*, we had *only* three *very* long classes. (3)

2. He *certainly* prepared the *extremely* detailed proposal *carefully*. (3)

3. Sue will *soon* begin her trip for her *much* needed vacation *home*. (3)

4. *Easily*, the *really* talented performer won the competition. (2)

5. The brothers have *not yet* decided to run in that race. (2)

6. They crept *very quickly away* from the large crowd. (3)

7. *Soon*, the *rather* slow turtle will *finally* cross the finish line. (3)

8. The president will *not* leave until *absolutely* the last guest has left, *too*. (3)

9. *Much later*, the group *quietly* returned to their *now* deserted headquarters. (4)

10. The children will *never ever* believe that *quite* unusual story. (3)

Quiz #12

1. *Someday*, we shall bring all of our *most* successful projects *in*. (3)

2. Nothing could *ever* convince them that they were included, *also*. (2)

3. *Happily*, the missing kitten was *quickly* found and brought *back*. (3)

4. That *most* interesting tool is *not yet* on the market *here*. (4)

5. *Sunday*, an *extremely* powerful sermon will be given *very early*. (4)

6. *Frequently*, a *much* smaller bus will be brought *over*. (3)

7. All of the players returned their *slightly* used uniforms *Monday*. (2)

8. *Today,* the *never before* seen design will be revealed. (3)

9. *Still* open, the store was letting customers *in* and *out*. (3)

10. She will *now* deliver books to *nearly* every library *there*. (3)

Section VI: SENTENCES

Chapter 18: Sentence or Fragment

In the following quizzes, students will determine whether each group of words is a sentence or a fragment. A sentence must have a subject (can be "understood"), a verb, and must express a complete thought. A list of phrases or an adverb clause does not constitute a sentence. An imperative sentence *can* be only one word (a verb).

No punctuation will be added in this section unless the group of words is a sentence. An "S" or an "F" at the end of each group of words will designate the classification. Students will write either an "S" or an "F."

Quiz #1

1. The boys walked slowly. (S)

2. Behind the bookcase in the hall (F)

3. Because it was raining (F)

4. To the store in the mall (F)

5. Please stop by the store. (S)

6. When the traffic had died down (F)

7. A pile of papers on the counter (F)

8. Around a bend in the road ahead (F)

9. He took his time selecting a gift. (S)

10. Although he was tired (F)

Quiz #2

1. A list from every student in the class (F)

2. By the man in the blue jacket (F)

3. Nothing could be heard. (S)

4. Stopping by the side of the road (F)

5. Because he wanted to go with us (F)

6. The two friends stood together. (S)

7. Jump. (S)

8. When the field had dried out (F)

9. Please carry your own suitcase. (S)

10. Several shelves of books near the door of the library (F)

Quiz #3

1. During the last class of the day (F)

2. Be careful! (S)

3. Even though the competition was over (F)

4. Beside a bench in the park (F)

5. Running down the empty street quickly (F)

6. He decided to finish his trip early. (S)

7. Please watch the signs. (S)

8. After it had snowed so hard (F)

9. Near a bicycle in the window of the store (F)

10. Concerned about her health (F)

Quiz #4

1. As the rain fell heavily on the soccer field (F)

2. No one in the main room (F)

3.   Stop! (S)

4.   By pulling the mask over his face (F)

5.   The small boat raced across the waves. (S)

6.   Although he knew the way (F)

7.   The old man could not remember him. (S)

8.   From where he stood, it was visible. (S)

9.   Pick a spot and wait. (S)

10. Along the edge of the hall (F)

Quiz #5

1.   Hold on to the wall. (S)

2.   The little boy in the red wagon (F)

3.   Because the room was extremely dark (F)

4.   It is never too late. (S)

5.   Since it was theirs (F)

6.   All the news was good. (S)

7.   When the noise had stopped (F)

8.   Near the entrance to the railroad tunnel (F)

9.   Although each boy knew the correct answer (F)

10. Then, they moved around the corner. (S)

Quiz #6

1.   When the sun had gone behind a cloud (F)

2.   Near the edge of the lake (F)

3.   A small boy ran by me. (S)

4.   With his head stuck out the window (F)

5. Run! (S)

6. As the bell rang loudly (F)

7. Nothing could stop them. (S)

8. Since the strong wind had started to blow (F)

9. They will be leaving later. (S)

10. Bring me a new book, please. (S)

Quiz #7

1. After they had stopped playing in the pool (F)

2. Near the backpack on the floor (F)

3. The cat and the dog stopped suddenly. (S)

4. In the light from the candle (F)

5. His whole arm ached. (S)

6. Before the next train could arrive from the city (F)

7. From the corner where he was standing (F)

8. It is a new model. (S)

9. With his book and papers ready to go (F)

10. Stop by the store on the way home. (S)

Quiz #8

1. Help him! (S)

2. On his bicycle through the pouring rain (F)

3. Next to the boy on the field (F)

4. Seeing is believing. (S)

5. Create a new one, please. (S)

6. Because all the lights in the house were out (F)

7.   When my parents arrive home (F)

8.   With a hole in the bottom of his left shoe (F)

9.   Everything matters to him. (S)

10.   The flowers on the table by the door to the kitchen (F)

Quiz #9

1.   He stopped early. (S)

2.   Because he wanted to win (F)

3.   Play hard. (S)

4.   When he quietly entered the room (F)

5.   Although he was sick with the flu (F)

6.   As we arrived, they were leaving. (S)

7.   By the front door to the gym (F)

8.   No one had seen him. (S)

9.   Run away! (S)

10.   Since I went home with him (F)

Quiz #10

1.   When the leaves began falling from the trees (F)

2.   Run home from my house. (S)

3.   From the man in the store on the corner (F)

4.   Even though it had turned dark outside (F)

5.   Come here! (S)

6.   The children picked cherries from the tree. (S)

7.   Over by the box in the corner of the room (F)

8. Certainly not tomorrow (F)

9. Under the watchful eyes of a very caring mother (F)

10. Because the boys knew all the answers (F)

Quiz #11

1. Call him tonight. (S)

2. Out of the stream in the woods by our house (F)

3. Even though she knew she was right (F)

4. When the first light of the morning sun hit the hilltops (F)

5. Stopping quickly at his house (F)

6. It was raining. (S)

7. Be careful with those dishes, please. (S)

8. Over the fence and into the back yard (F)

9. Through a broken window at the back of the garage (F)

10. Looking across the field toward the barn (F)

Quiz #12

1. Sailed into the wind (F)

2. Over the tops of the hills near the edge of the valley (F)

3. Face front! (S)

4. Nobody wanted dessert. (S)

5. As it started to hail (F)

6. Swimming across the pool very quickly (F)

7. Posters on every wall (F)

8.   There were three more contestants on the list. (S)

9.   Thrown from the pitcher's mound (F)

10. Suddenly, it ceased. (S)

Quiz #13

1.   Run steadily. (S)

2.   There was an eagle in the tree. (S)

3.   Someone must have left early. (S)

4.   As a loud bell rang in the distance (F)

5.   All the students from my class at school (F)

6.   Hoping to reach his home before dinner (F)

7.   She cried suddenly. (S)

8.   By the door to the side of the house (F)

9.   Because it was raining too hard for a game (F)

10. Let them come with us. (S)

Quiz #14

1.   After the snow had fallen all night (F)

2.   Please stop! (S)

3.   My friends are going also. (S)

4.   When all the shouting had stopped (F)

5.   In the bottom of a big hole in the middle of the yard (F)

6.   Because we needed a ride to the movie (F)

7.   Five girls played in the game. (S)

8.   Around a curve in the road up ahead (F)

9. Sitting on the bleachers in the gym (F)

10. The waves and the beautiful sandy shore (F)

Quiz #15

1. Under the window in the garden (F)

2. There were three robins on the limb. (S)

3. Please return that. (S)

4. Even though they had all agreed on the color (F)

5. Stranded in the middle of the storm (F)

6. Dishes on every empty square inch (F)

7. Easily, they had won. (S)

8. Near the middle of the third column on the page (F)

9. As soon as the wind dies down (F)

10. We would like to think about it. (S)

Quiz #16

1. Did you go? (S)

2. On the top shelf of the bookcase in the library (F)

3. As soon as he had arrived (F)

4. I shall soon return. (S)

5. Hanging on the wall near the door (F)

6. A long trail of ants (F)

7. When the team had entered the locker room (F)

8. Washed up on the shore (F)

9. Run ahead. (S)

10. Here on the kitchen counter (F)

Chapter 19: Four Types of Sentences According to Use

In the following quizzes, students will determine whether each sentence is *imperative*, *declarative*, *interrogative*, or *exclamatory*. To recognize an <u>exclamatory</u> sentence in an oral (or standardized test), students must listen (or look) for a *What a...* or a <u>*How...*</u> (not as an interrogative) beginning. An <u>imperative</u> sentence does not contain a subject; a "You" is understood but does not appear in the actual sentence. <u>Declarative</u> sentences are the most common and simply make a statement, and an <u>interrogative</u> sentence will always ask a question.

The type will be identified in parentheses after each sentence, and punctuation will also be shown. Students will write either <u>Exclamatory</u> (Exc.), <u>Declarative</u> (Dec.), <u>Interrogative</u> (Int.), or <u>Imperative</u> (Imp.).

Quiz #1

1. How beautiful she looks in her new gown! (Exc.)

2. Please help him with his homework. (Imp.)

3. No one could make it to the last meeting. (Dec.)

4. Put on a jacket before going into the cold. (Imp.)

5. Will your friends stay for dinner? (Int.)

6. All of the leaves had fallen from the trees. (Dec.)

7. Who will play second base? (Int.)

8. What a wonderful idea! (Exc.)

9. *Help! (Imp./Exc.)

10. Are you finished with your chores? (Int.)

Quiz #2

1. Stop by the store on the way home. (Imp.)

2. Don't you want to finish your dinner? (Int.)

3. I can carry that for you. (Dec.)

4. What a beautiful Christmas gift! (Exc.)

5. She read many books over the summer. (Dec.)

6. Can we attend the dance at school? (Int.)

7. How lovely your ring is! (Exc.)

8. That student likes to play all sports. (Dec.)

9. When will the others arrive? (Int.)

10. Control the game in the second half. (Imp.)

Quiz #3

1. Can you be here by 9 o'clock? (Int.)

2. None of them can go. (Dec.)

3. Bring me that book, please. (Imp.)

4. Do not show her that. (Imp.)

5. When will he come home from the mall? (Int.)

6. How interesting your speech was! (Exc.)

7. Did she run in all the races? (Int.)

8. What a perfect picture of you and your father! (Exc.)

9. Make at least three dozen cookies. (Imp.)

10. We can all arrive at the airport early. (Dec.)

Quiz #4

1. There were three books on the highest shelf. (Dec.)

2.   Send the package to your friend. (Imp.)

3.   How perfect the timing of the event was! (Exc.)

4.   Push, please. (Imp.)

5.   Didn't he enter the contest after you? (Int.)

6.   She will bring the receipt by later. (Dec.)

7.   Can she ride her bike over tomorrow? (Int.)

8.   The lamp in the living room was on. (Dec.)

9.   What a strange place for a park! (Exc.)

10. Who is the person on the telephone? (Int.)

Quiz #5

1.   Can you leave the reports on my desk? (Int.)

2.   How bright the morning sun is! (Exc.)

3.   She wandered around the neighborhood aimlessly. (Dec.)

4.   Return to the house immediately. (Imp.)

5.   Her mother pushed her on the swings. (Dec.)

6.   How did she get home from school? (Int.)

7.   Stop at each house for a donation. (Imp.)

8.   Couldn't she bring her brother with her? (Int.)

9.   What a glorious sunset! (Exc.)

10. She could not believe his story. (Dec.)

Quiz #6

1.   Never give up on your dreams. (Imp.)

2.   He is going to the movies tonight. (Dec.)

3.   When will he be home from school? (Int.)

4.   What a gorgeous centerpiece on your dining room table! (Exc.)

5.   Stop by my office on your way to the field. (Imp.)

6.   He always rides his bicycle to school. (Dec.)

7.   The wind was blowing leaves across the playground. (Dec.)

8.   How lovely she looks in her new dress! (Exc.)

9.   How many times did she call you last night? (Int.)

10. Return all the books to the library on time. (Imp.)

Quiz #7

1.   Please close the door on the way out to your car. (Imp.)

2.   We will return the books to the library tomorrow. (Dec.)

3.   What beautiful dresses the girls found for the event! (Exc.)

4.   When will they arrive home from their vacation? (Int.)

5.   Did you remember to bring the flowers? (Int.)

6.   My mother ordered all her gifts from that catalog. (Dec.)

7.   All the traffic was directed around the construction. (Dec.)

8.   How scared she appeared! (Exc.)

9.   Show them how to convert the money they brought. (Imp.)

10. Can you reach the jars on the top shelf? (Int.)

Quiz #8

1. How long did your homework take? (Int.)
2. Swim to the end of the pool. (Imp.)
3. I left school after the game was over. (Dec.)
4. Her friends are coming over for a visit. (Dec.)
5. What a marvelous evening we have had! (Exc.)
6. Will you play tennis Saturday afternoon? (Int.)
7. Start over at the beginning. (Imp.)
8. How comfortable everyone looks! (Exc.)
9. When will the rest of them arrive? (Int.)
10. Please send all of the important papers to me. (Imp.)

Quiz #9

1. Who brought the cookies to the party? (Int.)
2. Several men fished at the edge of the lake. (Dec.)
3. Should the coach cancel the game? (Int.)
4. What an exceptional project you have created! (Exc.)
5. Read all the instructions carefully. (Imp.)
6. Please write a letter to notify them of the results. (Imp.)
7. They drove to the park for the game. (Dec.)
8. What a great day for a picnic! (Exc.)
9. What name did you put on the reservation? (Int.)
10. We have extra tickets you can use. (Dec.)

Quiz #10

1. Oh, what a wonderful idea! (Exc.)

2. The woman in the car is my friend. (Dec.)

3. Can you stop at the store on the way home? (Int.)

4. Don't run across the street. (Imp.)

5. A pile of papers was on the corner of the desk. (Dec.)

6. Were you on time for the movie? (Int.)

7. Has the rain stopped? (Int.)

8. How strange the decorations looked! (Exc.)

9. Finish all of your vegetables. (Imp.)

10. My brother has a doctor's appointment today. (Dec.)

Chapter 20: Four Types of Sentences According to Structure

There are <u>four</u> types of sentences in English that are classified according to their structure. These sentences, *simple*, *compound*, *complex*, and *compound-complex*, are easy to recognize when separated into their parts. A SIMPLE sentence contains only one subject (may be compound) but may have a single or compound verb or predicate, including phrases. It has only *one* independent clause. A COMPOUND sentence contains two independent clauses (two subjects and verbs) but no dependent clauses. COMPLEX sentences consist of one independent clause and one or more dependent (adjective, adverb, or noun) clauses. A COMPOUND-COMPLEX sentence is one that is made up of two independent clauses (two subjects and two verbs) and one or more dependent clauses. In any of the four sentence types, adding adjectives, adverbs, phrases, or verbals (gerunds, participles, and infinitives) does not affect the structure.

In the quizzes that follow, all four types of sentences will be represented, and students will be required to write whether each is <u>Simple</u> (S), <u>Compound</u> (Cpd), <u>Complex</u> (Cx), or <u>Compound-complex</u> (C-c). To keep these oral quizzes short, the sentences will be very basic.

Quiz #1

1.   The boys and girls returned to school after the event. (S)

2.   When the weather turned cold, the pools closed their gates, and the parks were deserted. (C-c)

3. They could not come since they were out of town. (Cx)

4. As she arrived at the terminal, the last plane of the day was leaving. (Cx)

5. Several children climbed the fence and dropped to the other side. (S)

6. By the end of the day, the girls had won three games, and the boys had captured the title. (Cpd)

7. Nothing could change his mind, but he was willing to think about another procedure. (Cpd)

8. There were three winners when we were finished, and no one was unhappy with the results. (C-c)

9. Although he left home on time, the show had already begun. (Cx)

10. In the heat of the summer, the temperatures rise above one hundred and do not drop at night. (S)

Quiz #2

1. Before he could return the books, the library had issued him a fine. (Cx)

2. My mother and father bought snacks and sodas for our group. (S)

3. As the runners approached the finish line, three students from our school were in the front. (Cx)

4. If he returns, we shall complete the project, and then she can turn it in. (C-c)

5. They skipped through the forest, and the deer and squirrels watched from their hiding places. (Cpd)

6. We bought the groceries, and he took them home since we would not be going for a while. (C-c)

7. My younger sister called from her home in the mountains to wish us luck. (S)

8. On the racetrack the drivers were warming up, and the officials were ready to begin the race. (Cpd)

9. The boys rode their bikes, but the girls walked when they went to the park for the game. (C-c)

10. My friends and I brought many movies and refreshments for the party. (S)

Quiz #3

1. Could you bring your bicycle when you come to visit? (Cx)

2. Climbing the tree, the small boy arrived at his fort. (S)

3. The three children ran toward the park, but the others were already there. (Cpd)

4. To run the mile, the young man needed practice. (S)

5. As the road turned, the car slowed, and the occupants looked out the window. (C-c)

6. Even though she had made thirty sandwiches, the hungry youngsters wanted more. (Cx)

7. He showed his friends his trophy, and they were happy when they realized what he had done. (C-c)

8. My mother baked the cookies, and my sister made the punch. (Cpd)

9. Before the end of the movie, the children knew the solution to the mystery. (S)

10. As soon as she returned the keys, the others were ready to go. (Cx)

Quiz #4

1. After he had left, the girls locked all the doors. (Cx)

2. In the large cage, a beautiful parrot squawked loudly. (S)

3. Nothing was done correctly, and since no one knew how they could fix the problem, they waited. (C-c)

4. Did the parents and the students attend both of the meetings? (S)

5. The manager of the store offered him a job, and he quickly accepted it. (Cpd)

6. When the clouds had cleared and the field had dried, the softball game continued. (Cx)

7. As the picnic began, my sister finished her game of chess, and my brother stopped playing his game of basketball. (C-c)

8. It was a very good movie, and my best friend from school went with me to see it. (Cpd)

9. The large dogs were barking, and the fireworks were exploding overhead. (Cpd)

10. On their summer trip to Alaska, my parents and yours took many pictures and collected souvenirs. (S)

Quiz #5

1. At the beginning of the day, her sister runs three miles, and then she eats a delicious breakfast. (Cpd)

2. Starting at the beginning, she read the entire book aloud. (S)

3. When he arrives at school, my brother puts his things in his locker and goes to class. (Cx)

4. They ran around the track, and each of them finished the event as quickly as they could. (C-c)

5. There were three puppies for sale, and we picked the cutest one of the litter. (Cpd)

6. By the edge of the pool, a large group of teenagers listened to a friend playing his guitar. (S)

7. The group of scouts knew the area well although many had never been there before. (Cx)

8. We left the party, and my mother took us to the mall since it was still open. (C-c)

9. At the ice rink, the skaters practiced their routines and prepared for the competition on Saturday. (S)

10. The traffic on the freeway was heavy, and we arrived late at the party. (Cpd)

Quiz #6

1. She brought the supplies to school, and her friends finished the project that afternoon. (Cpd)

2. With his dog on a leash, the young boy walked quickly to the park. (S)

3. They could not enter the contest, for the members of the group were not old enough. (Cx)

4. The old clock on the wall had been moved, and a new, modern version was in its place. (Cpd)

5. The train's whistle warned the passengers on the platform of its approach. (S)

6. In the end of the story, the hero saves the princess, and they live happily ever after. (Cpd)

7. While the others in the group were playing basketball, we ordered pizza for everyone. (Cx)

8. The small dog ran across the yard when he saw his owner, but the cat continued to bathe in the sun. (C-c)

9. When the day was over, the judges had turned in their scores, and the winners had been selected. (C-c)

10. After the game had ended, the fans returned home and celebrated the victory. (Cx)

Quiz #7

1. In the middle of the night, a strong wind blew leaves and debris down the street. (S)

2. The rain pelted the roof, and the fire crackled in the fireplace as the children listened to their music. (C-c)

3. Until we know the exact time of the party, we will stay where they can call us. (Cx)

4. Can we arrive at the stadium before the game begins? (Cx)

5. Suddenly, at the head of the table, the host offered a toast to his guests. (S)

6. The judge entered the courtroom, and the jury and spectators rose. (Cpd)

7. My friend rides horses, and her brother races cars since cars are much faster. (C-c)

8. A very large bird flew into the pine tree, but no one spotted a nest. (Cpd)

9. They all saw the young girl who was the winner. (Cx)

10. With his friends on the team, my brother went to the pizza parlor after the game. (S)

Quiz #8

1. As soon as they choose a leader, we shall begin the conference. (Cx)

2. On Halloween the haunted house distributed candy and conducted scary tours. (S)

3. Along the coast large waves hit the rocks, and homes were threatened as the hurricane moved toward shore. (C-c)

4. The contestants and judges moved to the front of the stage. (S)

5. A mother and her son entered the room, but they soon turned around and left. (Cpd)

6. The librarian checked out the books when the students were ready to leave. (Cx)

7. That young man is the one who selected the subjects. (Cx)

8. These are the games which we chose, and we want to play them at the picnic. (C-c)

9. My sister finished the track meet, and then we called our parents. (Cpd)

10. He applied for the job, but it was given to the man who had more experience. (C-c)

Quiz #9

1. Although we knew the way, we still became lost. (Cx)

2. Last night my sister and brother arrived from college. (S)

3. The dogs barked, and the babies cried as the thunder rumbled across the sky. (C-c)

4. The schedule was changed yesterday, but new classes do not begin until next week. (Cpd)

5. The road was extremely rough, yet we continued to drive to the top of the ridge. (Cpd)

6. Those are the maps which the boys will follow. (Cx)

7. Soon, a new trail will lead to the top of the mountain and down the other side. (S)

8. These are the directions, and she is the guide who will lead us. (C-c)

9. You can come with us, or you can wait for them and come later. (Cpd)

10. Everyone in the play was excited when it was held over for another week. (Cx)

Quiz #10

1. The young boy and his friendly dog walked along the street toward town. (S)

2. That curvy road is the one which we will have to take. (Cx)

3. My mother and sister shopped the entire mall, but they could not find the vase. (Cpd)

4. The ushers seated us, and the game began just as the last lights came on. (C-c)

5. Since their names were at the top of the list, they were seated first. (Cx)

6. She has bred different types of dogs over the years but prefers golden retrievers. (S)

7. The group will either arrive on time, or they will not come at all. (Cpd)

8. In the morning my friends and I will leave for camp, and our parents will pick us up in a week. (Cpd)

9. He is the owner of the building that we rented, and he does not care if we paint it. (C-c)

10. At the circus the clowns, elephants, and tigers thoroughly entertained the audience of children and adults. (S)

Chapter 21: Conclusion

Although the English language is difficult to master, the use of the quizzes in this book on a regular, repetitive basis will make a noticeable difference in fundamental comprehension. Students learn through repetition, and it is with that theory in mind that each section has numerous quizzes to help students master the concepts. Keeping the activity short and simple lessens student resistance and requires little instructor time commitment. This book, although not totally inclusive of all aspects of grammar, provides a solid foundation of English grammar basics for middle grade students of all academic levels.

About Abigail Hilson

Abigail Hilson is a 35-year veteran of teaching English to middle school and high school students. She has a Bachelor's Degree in English from Stanford University and a Master's Degree in English from the University of Nevada, Las Vegas. Abigail has taught in Texas, California, and Nevada, and has received numerous awards and accolades through the years, including being recognized as a Master Teacher and being honored in a television spot as an outstanding educator. Her peers refer to her as the *go-to* person for English grammar and punctuation questions. The lessons in this book have helped thousands of students achieve a greater comprehension of the English language. Abigail recently retired after teaching English for 26 years at the well-known Meadows School in Las Vegas, receiving a special proclamation from the mayor for her years of dedication and excellence in teaching English.

Order Form

For individual copies of this book:

www.Amazon.com

For resale case lot orders, contact your local book wholesaler through Ingram or Baker & Taylor.

For speaking and seminar opportunities, or additional teaching materials, contact Abigail through her website:

www.TheHomeschoolEnglishTeacher.com

www.ingramcontent.com/pod-product-compliance
Lightning Source LLC
LaVergne TN
LVHW051500080426
835509LV00017B/1836